How to Serve Humanity

Wielding the Law of Relationship

Additional works by Glen Knape
available from Preparation Press:

The Aquarian Christ

The Ashram of Syntheses

The Knight of the Temple

The Magic of Consciousness, Workshops

The Nature of The Soul Study Guide and Practice Manual

Raising the Queen of Heaven

Further information on these and other works is
available at: www.preparationpress.com

How to Serve Humanity

Wielding the Law of Relationship

By Glen Knape

Preparation Press
Concord, CA

How to Serve Humanity

Wielding the Law of Relationship

by Glen Knape

First edition, 2011

Preparing the way

Preparation Press
Concord, CA, USA

Cover Art: "Aladin Sky" by Lucette Bourdin,
http://www.lbourdin.com/

ISBN 978-0-9834188-0-1 $16.95

VIII

Prelude

We are blessed to live at a time of unequalled opportunity; a time when humanity is beginning to awaken to our true nature. If we collectively and individually accept this opportunity, then humanity will finally recognize its true place and take up its function in the planetary life. Earth will not only be saved from our destructive behavior, but will blossom with beauty and harmony.

While this sounds like a utopian dream, it is true, nevertheless, and each of us can contribute to it—by our inner and outer action.

The consequences of failing to act are obvious: a rising tide of mass extinctions, epidemics, displaced populations, hunger, thirst... the list seems endless. Yet all of these crises are, in a greater sense, part of the current opportunity. They drive us to become aware of the consequences of our actions, that we *must* change, and that we *can* change.

That change will be brought about by the right understanding and use of the "laws" by which the world works. There are many such laws, some more important or easier to use than others, and much has been said recently about some of them, particularly those that enable one to consciously recreate the world around us.

What is often overlooked, however, is that the ability to be consciously creative does not, in itself, determine the effects of one's creative activity on the greater planetary life. Those effects are determined by other laws, such as the *Law of Relationship*.

The Law of Relationship is also known as the Law of Magnetism and the Law of Polarity. This Law relates our creative activity (inner and outer) with our motivating purpose, and our motivating purpose with our creative activity, bringing them into a condition of union or at-one-ment. As a result, our motive or intent is an inherent part of the creative process and is largely responsible for the effects of that process.

If our motive is part of the purpose of the planetary life, then the result of our creative activity will be in harmony with that life.

If our motive is not part of the purpose of the planetary life, but separate from it, then the result will be disharmony within that life.

This series shows how to use the Law of Relationship to discover our purpose within the planetary life, and help serve humanity and save Earth. This process begins with the following inner alignment...

Harmony Through At-one-ment

With the Planetary Life

"Sit comfortably with your back straight, your feet flat on the floor and your arms on the chair's armrests or in your lap (not crossed).

"Close your eyes and relax your physical body – beginning with your toes and moving upward to your head, command each portion to relax. Imagine a soothing warmth, a tingling sensation, golden light, or whatever other method works for you.

"Slowly relax your toes... your feet... ankles... forelegs... knees... thighs... buttocks... tummy... lower back... diaphragm... upper back... chest and heart... fingers... hands... forearms... upper arms... shoulders... neck... tongue... scalp... the muscles of the face... and the muscles behind the eyes.

"Move your self awareness into your heart (If it helps, you may picture a tiny version of yourself standing within a sphere of golden-white light in the middle of your chest).

"From your position in the heart, imagine lines of golden light moving out from you, linking you with every one and every thing in the planetary life.

"Become aware that you are part of that life, that you exist within it.

"Feel that awareness grow as you become one with that life.

"When that awareness reaches its height, take a deep breath, relax your attention, and slowly open your eyes."

XII

Introduction

We are blessed to live at a time of awakening, when humanity is forcing itself to create solutions to its many problems. This task often appears insurmountable, for no mater how hard we try it seems our every effort is met with opposition and conflict.

This conflict is the natural and normal result of the Law of Relationship. When we understand that Law, and wield it in service to humanity and the planetary life, opposition disappears and conflicts dissolve.

The Law is extremely simple, and practicing it is a normal and natural part of being human. Usually we practice the Law unconsciously, and our effects are quite limited. As we become more self-aware, we practice the Law more consciously, and our creative activities become increasingly effective.

At first our motives are quite self-centered, focused on our personal appetites and slowly progressing to include the needs of our family, friends, business, or community—the people and things we've identified with and become attached to.

This is normal. Human beings naturally progress from the needs of infancy to the responsibilities of adulthood. However, whenever we create from a self-centered motive (creating for my self, my family, my business, etc.), that motive is isolated from and out of harmony with the planetary life, and the results will be detrimental to that life. This is inevitable, because motive or intent is part of the Law and helps determine the effects of all creative activity.

How to Serve Humanity

Our self awareness or identity is also part of the Law. Most human beings become aware of their self, as an individual, sometime around age two. From then on, when we look into a mirror we see our individual self. This is a normal stage in the development of humanity, and is the source of our ability to relate with others as individuals—"I am over here, you are over there".

However, whenever we create from a *self-centered identity* (*my* self, *my* family, *my* business, etc.), that identity is isolated from and out of harmony with the planetary life, and the results will be detrimental to that life. This is inevitable, because self awareness or identity is part of the Law and helps determine the effects of all creative activity.

Our inner and outer activity is also part of the Law. Most human beings develop sophisticated emotional, and mental abilities, as well as physical. This is normal and natural, and the source of our ability to focus and empower our outer activity.

However, whenever our creative activity is motivated by self interest and directed by separative identity that activity is out of harmony with the planetary life, and the results will be detrimental to that life. This is inevitable because activity is part of the Law and helps determine the effects of the Law.

These are the three aspects of the Law of Relationship— the motivating purpose of Spirit, the relationship of Consciousness, and the creative activity of Matter. When our purpose is part of the planetary purpose, when our identity is part of the planetary self, when our activity is a dedicated part of the planetary activity, then

2

the effects will be in harmony with the planetary life.

When our motivating purpose, our identity, and our activity are within but separate from that life, then the results reflect that separation. This is the situation for most of humanity today, but it will not remain so for this is a time of Awakening!

* * *

In order to wield the Law of Relationship to the benefit of the planetary life, rather than to its detriment, we must change. Up to now, this evolutionary leap (sometimes called enlightenment, cosmic consciousness, or at-one-ment) has been taken by individuals. However, our many problems, the products of our selfish creative activity, are forcing humanity to change *as one*.

We have created the opportunity for all of us to take that evolutionary leap together. If we do so, from then on every member of humanity will be aware of themselves as both an individual within the human kingdom, and as part of the one planetary life. Our purpose will be part of the planetary purpose, our consciousness will be part of the planetary consciousness, and our creative activity will be part of the planetary activity.

All of this is made not only possible, but necessary, by the many problems and difficulties we have created. We have placed our self in the position where the only way to solve our problems is by applying the Law of Relationship in service to the one planetary life. That practical application of the Law in service is the process by which we will take the leap into at-one-ment.

The first step in resolving a problem is to recognize that *we* have one. The next is to take responsibility for that problem. However, because of our individual motives and identity, we are unable to do either properly.

Our individual identity isolates us from the rest of the planetary life. This isolation was a necessary stage in the evolution of humanity. It enabled us to develop capacities (mental, emotional, etc.) that we need in order to perform our function in the planetary life, and which we would not otherwise have had. However, it is a stage in our evolution, not the goal, and its consequences are forcing us to awaken to the greater life of which we are a part.

As isolated individuals, we automatically divide things into that which is "mine" (*my* idea, *my* feeling, *my* hunger), and that which is "not mine" (*their* idea, *their* feelings, *their* hunger). The same consciousness that identifies a book as "mine" or a house as "theirs" identifies a problem as "mine" or "theirs." As we shall see, this is an illusion, and the results are always harmful to the individuals involved and to the planetary life.

We are all, each and every one of us, part of that one planetary life. We are all connected within that life, and what affects any one of us affects all of us. The appearance of isolated problems, individual or group, is an illusion created by the isolation of the separated self. As discussed later, it is not "my" problem or "your" problem. It is a condition within humanity that you have recognized because you have a relationship with it.

As lone individuals, we feel helpless before the larger life. This is a correct assessment. When we isolate ourselves from the one planetary life, we limit our creative potential. Our motivating power, ability to relate, and creative activity are restricted to those of our individual mind, emotions, and body.

Individuals react to these apparent limits in a number of ways. Many feel that they are powerless to change the world around them and thus are not responsible for the world's problems. However, this illusion merely disempowers them further as it robs them of the ability to respond creatively and effectively.

When we reject responsibility for a problem we renounce our *ability to respond,* to create change. How can we, when we have given away our creative power?

Some react by aspiring to become powerful enough to shape the world around them according to their own motives, thoughts, and feelings. This is natural and necessary, for, as we shall see, a strong individual identity is required for the next step in evolution. However, as we shall also see, as we develop the clarity of our individual mind, the power of our individual feelings, and the abilities of our individual body, we intensify the negative effects of our creative actions.

When we experience our self as part of the planetary life, that union expands our ability to move within and influence that life. The motivating power, ability to relate, and creative activity available to us is unlimited. We then recognize all problems as our problems, and take responsibility for them.

Fortunately, there is a way to transition from destructive individual motives to benevolent, inclusive motives. One begins by accepting that one is both an individual and part of a collective consciousness. Then, in aspiration to the one life of which one is a part, one wields the Law of Relationship in service to that life.

This is how we consciously take the next step in our spiritual growth and development—awaken to our purpose and place, and take up our function within the one planetary life.

All of this is made possibly by the conscious, focused, and persistent use of the Law of Relationship.

The Law of Relationship

The following pages offer the opportunity to perform and study the Law of Relationship. When you take up the Law, and what you do with it, is entirely up to you. However, having read these pages, you will no longer be able to proceed in ignorance. You will no longer be able to claim that you are powerless, that you are not able to respond to the problems that surround you. You will have the power to create whatsoever you will.

The Law of Relationship gives us the power to create because it is power. It is the motivating power of Spirit, the relationship of Consciousness, and the creative activity of Matter. Utilizing these three, "Spirit," "Consciousness," and "Matter," it is possible to define the Law as follows:

> *Everything that exists, in order to exist, must be three things—a motivating purpose, a relating consciousness, and an expressing activity.*[1]

---

[1] The Law of Relationship is virtually identical to the scientific "Law of Electromagnetism." The basic elements are the

6

Introduction

The source of motivating purpose is sometimes called *"Spirit"* or the first aspect of divinity. The planetary spirit is the source of the purpose, power, and will of the entire planetary life. The planetary purpose includes the purpose of every kingdom in nature (mineral, plant, animal, and human) and of every individualized soul within that life.

Likewise, the planetary power and will include the power and will of every kingdom in nature, and of every individualized soul within the planetary life. Thus, our individual will is part of the will of the planetary life. As we awaken, we become aware that our purpose, power, and will are part of, rather than separate from, that of the one life. Our purpose, power, and will are seen and experienced as a portion of the planetary will—a portion with which we are related and for which we are responsible.

We will discuss the purpose, power, and will of Spirit in more detail as we proceed. However, our focus will be on aligning our individual purpose with planetary purpose, our power with planetary power, and our will with planetary will, and acting in the world from that alignment.

The source of creative activity is sometimes called *"Matter"* or the third aspect of divinity. The planetary matter is the source of energy, force, and activity of the entire planetary life. It is the stuff of which everything is made, including the mental thoughts, emotional feelings, and electric patterns of every kingdom in nature and of every individualized soul within that life.

---

same, but where the Law of Electromagnetism describes the characteristics of electromagnets, the Law of Relationship describes the basic characteristics of everything that exists.

Thus, our individual matter (including our energy, force, and forms) is part of the matter of the planetary life. As we awaken, we become aware that our thoughts, feelings, and actions are part of, rather than separate from, that of the one life. Our thoughts, feelings, and actions are seen and experienced as a portion of the planetary matter—a portion with which we are closely related and for which we are responsible.

We will discuss the energy, force, and activity of Matter in more detail as we proceed. However, our focus will be on aligning our energy, force, and activity with planetary will.

The second aspect of the Law is sometimes called "*Consciousness*" or "*Soul*." The planetary consciousness is the magnetic field of relationship between the Spirit and Matter of the one life. It is the identity or self awareness of everything in that life, including the soul of every kingdom in nature and of every individualized soul within that life.

Thus, our individual self is part of the one soul of the planetary life. As we awaken, we become aware that our individual consciousness is part of, rather than separate from, that of the one consciousness. Our individual identity is not lost, but experienced as a portion of the planetary consciousness—a portion with a purpose, place, and function within that life.

We will discuss consciousness in more detail as we proceed. However, our focus will be on identifying as soul within the one life, and relating purpose with matter and matter with purpose, so that the two poles become one. This is the Law in action, the creative process through which we serve humanity and the one life.

Introduction

The Creative Process

Each and all of us practice the Law, and are responsible for the results. When we are ignorant of the Law, and wield it unconsciously, we cannot see the relationship between our individual purpose and its effects in our life and affairs. But, we are still responsible for our role in creating that life. When we are aware of the Law, and wield it consciously, the relationship between our will and our life is obvious.

When you wield the Law consciously, you can no longer deny responsibility. You are aware of what you are doing when you wield it, and can see the results in your life and affairs. You then feel response-able—both empowered and accountable.

If you continue to act from selfish motives, that accountability becomes a heavy weight. A normal reaction is to attempt to justify our motives by creating reasons or excuses for why we think, feel, and act selfishly. However, the consequences of our behavior eventually reveal the delusion of those justifications.

If you fail to act, to help the world when you know you can, that responsibility festers. A normal reaction is to create reasons why we cannot act *now*. We tell ourselves that we would serve "if only"—if only we had the time, if only the children were grown, if only we knew what to do... However, the consequences of failing to act eventually reveal this disempowering delusion.

When you act as part of and for the benefit of the greater life, that responsibility empowers you. A normal initial response is to create an outer service activity—

something our personality finds interesting, attractive, and satisfying. We tell ourselves that whatever we are ready to do, that we enjoy doing, or that no one else is doing, must be *our* service activity. However, if the inner creative process is not performed first (relating a problem with the overshadowing planetary purpose, and that purpose with the embodied condition), then the service activity will not be in harmony with the planetary life.

Thus, the first step in finding our purpose and taking up our function within the planetary life is to perform the creative process.

The first step in the creative process is also a step in awakening to one's true self—the consciousness or soul. Having long been identified with our individual thoughts, feelings, and sensations, we slowly realize that our thoughts, feelings, and sensations are not ours alone, but part of those of a greater life of which we are a part.

This awareness may dawn slowly, burst forth in a mystical realization, or arise through mental exercise. Those reading these pages are almost certainly aware of the planetary life to some extent, and are likely seeking their place and function within that life. That place and function is your birthright—part of who and what you are.

The quest for your place and function within the greater life begins closer to home, with your place and method of function within your individual life. You begin the greater journey with a short one—discovering where you, the conscious thinking "I" dwell within your body.

Introduction

Discovering where you reside within your body is quite easy; if you can ignore any preconceptions you may have and look within. The following simple exercise will help you locate your self:

> Find a quite place, where you will not be disturbed and can sit comfortably. Sit with your back straight, your feet flat on the floor and your arms on the armrests or in your lap (not crossed).

> Close your eyes and relax your physical body, beginning with your toes and moving upward to your head. You may command each portion to relax, imagine a soothing warmth or tingling sensation, or use whatever other method works for you.

> Include every portion of your body, paying special attention to your tummy, diaphragm, heart, and neck.

> Recognize that wherever there is tension within your body, there your attention (a portion of your awareness) is being held.

> Sense all those points of attention within your body, and recognize which of them is strongest.

> Having recognized that strongest point of awareness, point to that place.

> Take a deep breath, and slowly open your eyes.

We have just located the *predominant* point where you, the conscious thinking 'I' reside within your physical form. However, it is not the *only* point. As we shall see, where you dwell within your body is not fixed. It is not only possible to move your awareness from one place in your body to another, but most of us do it all the time.

On a typical day we may place our inner point of attention in any of a number of locations (such as our tummy, diaphragm, heart, throat, and head), experiencing a different type of awareness in each. We will observe these various states of consciousness, including the purpose and function of each state, as we learn to perform the creative process.

Remember our definition of the Law of Relationship?

"Everything that exists, in order to exist, must be three things—a motivating purpose, a relating consciousness, and an expressing activity."

Thus, every state of awareness or quality of consciousness must also have motivating will and expressing matter.

Every quality of consciousness is overshadowed by its portion of the planetary spirit. That spirit is the source of the purpose, power, and will of that consciousness, and (like a magnetic field, moving energy from one magnetic pole to another) the consciousness relates that purpose to matter.

Thus, consciousness relates spirit to itself.

Every quality of consciousness relates its portion of planetary spirit to matter. The matter is motivated by the purpose, power, and will of spirit into new activity. This is how new thoughts, feelings, and ways of being are born in the world, but, as we shall see, it is also when the consciousness may identify with and become trapped in the form.

12

Introduction

Thus, consciousness relates spirit to matter.

Every quality of consciousness relates its portion of planetary matter to itself. This slowly transforms the mind, emotions, and body from a prison into an instrument of the consciousness.

Thus, consciousness relates matter to itself.

Every quality of consciousness relates its portion of planetary matter to spirit. This slowly transforms the self or soul into an identified portion of the one planetary soul.

Thus consciousness relates matter to spirit.

This natural, normal, everyday activity of your consciousness is the Law of Relationship in action.

Your consciousness relates spirit to itself, then

Your consciousness relates spirit to matter, then

Your consciousness relates matter to itself, then

Your consciousness relates matter to spirit.

It is a simple, creative process that we all perform automatically just by being self aware. Most of humanity performs this process unconsciously, with no real thought, direction, or control.

However, when we become aware that we can choose our state of consciousness, and thus relate a particular portion of the planetary purpose with a particular portion of matter, then we can create consciously, in full waking awareness.

How to Serve Humanity

The conscious creative process is nothing more, or less, than placing oneself in a particular state of consciousness and relating with the poles of spirit and matter. As one unites spirit and matter within one's self, that unity is reflected in the outer world. Our daily life and affairs, and the world around us, then reflect the harmony and at-one-ment of the one life.

Utilizing the following techniques, we will learn how to create at-one-ment. We will learn how to recognize the inner misrelationship (between spirit, matter, and consciousness) behind any outer problem, and how to create a solution to that problem via right relationship. We will learn how each and all of us, working together, can help awaken humanity and save Earth.

As the above suggests, awareness *is* response-ability. The more you become aware of *who* you are—of your purpose, place, and function within the planetary life—the more responsible you are for taking your place and performing your function within that life. While you will have the aid and companionship of many who share your purpose, function, and response-ability, the way will not be easy. Most refuse the opportunity many times before accepting the challenge, and awakening to the joy, of the one life. This also, is part of the path.

If you are ready, then let us begin.

Section 1

The Crisis of Awakening

How to Serve Humanity

Chapter 1

Awakening Your Purpose

We are blessed to live at a time of awakening, when humanity is forcing itself to create solutions to its many problems. This task often appears insurmountable, for no mater how hard we try it seems our every effort is met with opposition and conflict.

This conflict is the natural and normal result of the Law of Relationship. When we understand that Law, and wield it in service to humanity and the planetary life, opposition disappears and conflicts dissolve.

The Law is extremely simple, and practicing it is a normal and natural part of being human. Usually we practice the Law unconsciously, and our effects are quite limited. As we become more self-aware, we practice the Law more consciously, and our creative activities become increasingly effective.

At first our motives are quite self-centered, focused on our personal appetites and slowly progressing to include the needs of our family, friends, business, or community—the people and things we've identified with and become attached to.

This is normal. Human beings naturally progress from the needs of infancy to the responsibilities of adulthood. However, whenever we create from a *self-centered motive* (creating for *my* self, *my* family, *my* business, etc.), that motive is isolated from and out of harmony with the planetary life, and the results will be detrimental to that life. This is inevitable, because motive or intent is part of the Law and helps determine the effects of all creative activity.

The Conscious thinking "I"

We began our quest by locating where you, the conscious thinking "I" dwell within your body. You continue the quest by recognizing that you are the consciousness that dwells in the body. While you reside within the body, and may move from place to place within it, you are not that body.

This idea may seem simple and obvious, or abstract and difficult. It will tend to appear obvious if you have already experienced it as a reality. It will tend to appear abstract if you have not yet experienced it.

The following exercise will help you recognize your self as a consciousness that has a body:

> Sit comfortably with your back straight, your feet flat on the floor and your arms on the chair's armrests or in your lap.

> Close your eyes and relax your physical body – beginning with your toes and moving upward to your head, command each portion to relax. Imagine a soothing warmth, a tingling sensation, golden light, or whatever other method works for you.

> Slowly relax your toes... your feet... ankles... forelegs... knees... thighs... buttocks... tummy... lower back... diaphragm... upper back... chest and heart...

fingers... hands... forearms... upper arms... shoulders... neck... tongue... scalp... the muscles of the face... and the muscles behind the eyes.

Move into that point of strongest tension where you, the conscious thinking "I" spend most of your time within your body.

Recognize that you are the consciousness, residing in that place, in that body, just as you reside in your outer home (house, apartment, or condo).

Having recognized your consciousness as your true self or identity, take a deep breath and slowly open your eyes."

We have just identified our true self as the consciousness, thinking "I" that resides in the body. As we shall see, just as where you dwell within your body is not fixed, neither is your state of consciousness or awareness. It is possible to alter your state of awareness, and most of us do it all the time.

Chapter 1 Commentary

Part A

We are blessed to live at a time when the corrosive effects of our selfish motives are being revealed, and we are being forced to change. No matter how much we deny, bargain, or blame, this truth remains—we are all, each and every one of us, part of the one planetary life.

That life may be compared to a great, planetary organism—a planetary being with spiritual motives, self awareness, and inner thought, feeling and activity.

The motivating purpose of every life is determined by its place and function within the greater life of which it is a part. The human heart, for instance, supports the entire body by circulating blood. As long as it performs its function well, the entire body can prosper. If the heart performs its function poorly, then the entire body suffers.

So long as each of its muscle strands, valves, veins and arteries perform their function, the heart can prosper. If the cells in the pulse point fail to respond properly to motivating impulses from the brain, then the heart, and body, suffers.

In a sense, every kingdom in nature—mineral, plant, animal, and human—is an organ within the one planetary life. But within that life, the human kingdom is unique in several ways:

We exist within the same larger life as the other kingdoms, and share that life with them. In addition, some portion of each kingdom—mineral, plant, and animal—exists within us, and shares our life with us. Thus, because we are part of the one, and because the many are part of us, what we do has a more direct and powerful effect on all other parts of the planetary life.

We are self aware. Every human being is normally and naturally aware of themselves as a distinct individual. Like plants and animals, we can recognize another member of our species, and gender within that species. However, we are also aware of our self as an individual consciousness, and can become aware of our self as our kingdom. Thus, humanity has a range of self awareness unmatched by any other kingdom, and our ability to wield the Law of Relationship is much greater than that of any other kingdom.

We have become so identified with our individual personas that we have forgotten our true nature. We are consciousness or soul. We created personas that could think, feel, and act in the outer world, moved into those personas, and identified with them. And the moment we identified as the persona, we took on its abilities, and limits, and forgot our selves. We have wandered ever since, lost to our self and our purpose within the planetary life.

We *can* achieve liberation from the form. Human beings have the capacity, via consistent and persistent practice of the Law of Relationship, to achieve at-one-ment with the one planetary life, experience enlightenment, and thus liberate their self from the form. This has been the goal of individual seekers for many long ages. Many seek it today—following the examples of the great sages and saints who have gone before us. Yet, that is no longer our path.

How to Serve Humanity

The path before us today is the liberation of humanity.

This task may appear daunting, but we can accomplish it. The second step, after recognizing the challenge before us, is to realize that the obstacles we have created for ourselves are all, each and every one, opportunities for growth and development. Every crisis is an opportunity.

We can overcome all the obstacles we place in our way, awaken to our self, and at-one with the planetary life. We can do it by wielding the Law of Relationship to create solutions for those problems. We can do it because *we* created those obstacles.

We chose, as a kingdom, to evolve from species awareness to individuality. This gave us the unique capacity to wield the Law of Relationship as individuals.

As individuals, each of us identified with a portion of the planetary spirit, related with only that portion, and made it our own. Thus, each of us has our "own" motivating purpose, power, and will.

As individuals, each of us identified as a portion of the planetary consciousness or soul, related with only that portion, and made it our own. Thus, each of has our "own" identity, and we relate with our self and each other as separate beings.

As individuals, each of us identifies with portions of the planetary matter, relate with those portions, and make them our own. Thus, each of us has our "own" mental thoughts, emotional feelings, vital energy, and physical body, and we experience each other through isolated personas.

Chapter 1

We are choosing, as a kingdom, to evolve from individuality to kingdom awareness.

Via experience of the frustration and conflict of individual will, we slowly turn to larger purpose and motives. We identify with the goals of our family, community, nation, and planet, and make them our own. We merge our individual purpose with that of ever-greater portions of the one life, and experience the purpose, power, and will of that life. Thus, we align "our" motivating purpose with that of the greater life, and experience the harmony of that life.

Via experience of the loneliness and grief of individuality, we slowly turn to the larger identity of which we are a part. We identify with and as the consciousness of a group, community, or nation, and eventually with humanity as a whole. We do not lose our present self, but become an individual soul at-oned with the soul of humanity. As our consciousness grows, we expand our ability to relate with every portion of that life. Where the dreaming separate self relates "its" purpose with "its" matter, the awakened consciousness relates a portion of the planetary purpose with a portion of planetary matter. Thus, by adjusting our self awareness, we align separated will and matter, and reunite them within the one planetary life.

Via experience of the illusion of individual personas, each of us slowly learns that, although we have a physical body, we are not that body. Although we have emotional feelings, we are not those feelings. Although we have mental thoughts, we are not those thoughts. Although we may integrate our body, emotions, and mind into a single persona, we are not that persona. We are a consciousness that has a persona. We do not lose or abandon our persona, but recognize it as part of the matter of the planetary life—a portion for which we are directly and immediately responsible, and which gives us the ability to help manifest the purpose of the planetary life. Slowly, through practice of the Law of Relationship, we transform our persona into an instrument of the awakened soul. Thus, each of us has our "own" laboratory for precipitating divine will into appearance in the outer world.

We, as a kingdom, have created a world in which we must awaken in order to survive! Thus, survival is the motivation we chose, and because we are responsible for this world, we can transform it.

Chapter 1 Commentary

Part B

Motivation

In the Introduction we defined the Law of Relationship as follows:

"Everything that exists, in order to exist, must be three things—a motivating purpose, a relating consciousness, and an expressing activity."

Because everything is a formulation of Spirit, Consciousness, and Matter, a change to any one of the three will change the entire thing. Thus, when wielding the Law of Relationship, you:

> Align with a motivating purpose, in order to change the identity and the form of that purpose.

> Identify with and as a state of consciousness, in order to change the purpose and the form of that consciousness.

> Align with a form, in order to transform the spirit and consciousness overshadowing that form.

If everything that exists, in order to exist, must have purpose (a spark of spirit) within it, then the fact that something exists indicates that it has a purpose.

> The planetary life has a purpose, place, and function

within the greater life of which it is a part.

Humanity has a purpose, place, and function within the planetary life.

You have a purpose, place, and function within humanity.

So, how do you discover your purpose within humanity? Every human being normally and naturally has many motives—physical, emotional, and mental—but those are motives of our separated persona, and not of our self or soul.

Our soul is motivated by our spirit, a fragment of the spirit of the planetary life. We temporarily lose our alignment with our spiritual purpose when we move into and identify with our developing persona. We regain our alignment with and awareness of our spiritual purpose as we identify with our self or soul.

When we are born into the material world, we move into and identify with a physical body. When our body is hungry, we experience that appetite as our own. The appetite of the body becomes our motive, and we respond with physical activities such as crying and suckling. Motivated by our physical appetites, we spent the next several years exploring our body, developing it, learning to be in it.

Sometime around age two, we gazed into a mirror and recognized the image therein as a reflection of our self. The fact that we could recognize our self indicated we had a self. The identification with our body remained, as did our physical appetites. Yet, within and as that physical form we had become a self aware individual. With the new, additional, motivation of our dawning self awareness, we spent the following years exploring and developing that separated self.

About the time we began school, our focus shifted to our emotional desires. The identification with our physical body and appetites remained. Yet within and as that form we became increasingly aware of and identified with our emotions. With the additional motivation of our blossoming feelings, we spent the following years exploring and developing our emotions.

Sometime around the beginning of high school, we had the opportunity to begin developing our intellect or concrete rational mind. The identification with our body and emotions remained, as did their motives. Yet, we became increasingly aware of our thoughts, and interested in and receptive to "new" ideas. With the additional motivation of our dawning mind, we spent the following years exploring the realm of ideas and developing our thought process.

Eventually, when our body, emotions, and mind are fully developed, we have the opportunity to integrate them into a single, coherent persona. Up until then:

A part of us is identified with our body, and when the body is hungry we are hungry. That is the consciousness and part of the motive of our physical body.

A part of us is identified with our emotional feelings, and when our emotional instrument feels sad we feel sad. That is the consciousness and part of the motive of our emotional instrument.

A part of us is identified with our mental instrument, and every thought that passes through our mind we experience as *our* thought. That is the consciousness and motive of the mental instrument.

Each of these three aspects of the persona—physical body, emotional instrument, and mental instrument—has a number of motives. These motives often conflict with each other. Two conflicting motives are polar opposites. The motives work in opposition to each other, producing conflict and chaos.

Opposing motives within the physical body produce physical tension and conflict.

Opposing motives within the emotional feeling nature produce emotional tension and conflict.

Opposing motives within the mind produce mental tension and conflict.

In addition, the motives of each aspect are seldom in harmony with the motives of the other instruments (such as when a desire to lose weight conflicts with a powerful appetite for chocolate cheesecake). These opposing motives within the persona produce tension and conflict throughout the persona—body, emotions, and mind.

The resulting conflict in motives and actions forces us, as we grow and develop, to learn control.

We learn to control our appetites with our emotions. For instance, we may use our emotional desire for a more ideal form to suppress our appetite for chocolate cheesecake. However, emotional suppression of

Chapter 1

our appetites is only a temporary solution. Since the two are opposed to each other, the eventual result must be conflict.

We learn to suppress our appetites and emotions with our intellect. For instance, we may wield our mind like a vice, to still and contain our physical passions and emotional desires, or we may use our intellect to avoid the consequences of those appetites and emotions (such as a pill, to avoid the natural consequences of sex). However, intellectual suppression of our appetites and emotions is only a temporary solution. The appetites, emotions, and intellect still oppose each other, and the eventual result must be conflict.

Thus, as we grow and develop we naturally move from one identity ("I am my physical body," "I am my emotions," "I am my thoughts"), and one method of handling conflict, to another. Eventually, we force ourselves to recognize that:

We are not our bodies, and suppressing the appetites of the body does not work.

We are not our emotions, and suppressing our feelings does not work.

We are not our thoughts, and our intellect is incapable of solving our problems.

This is where humanity is today. We have created a world of conflict by creating conflict within our selves— by becoming that conflict.

Tension and conflict hold the attention of the indwelling consciousness, and trap it, within that portion of the persona and within that dwelling place in the instrument. As long as we remain identified as the separated self, every state of awareness, and every dwelling place within the instrument, is a place of conflict. As long as we identify with the separated persona, we will continue to create conflict in the world.

As we identify with and as the soul within the one planetary life, our entire persona (every portion of it) becomes a functional part of the body of the planetary life. It is not just "our" persona; it is a vehicle of harmony within the one life.

The Law of Relationship is the way to freedom from conflict. The Law enables us to awaken to the soul, our higher self, to align as soul with our purpose within the one planetary life, and to align that purpose with the conflict.

It does not matter if the conflict appears in the physical world, in the emotional realm, or in the mental. It does not matter if the conflict appears to be within ourselves, our family, neighborhood, or community. We can transform those conflicts by wielding the Law of Relationship.

As stated earlier, in the Law, purpose is the pole that motivates matter into action. When purpose is related to matter, matter responds by formulating itself into thoughts, feelings, activities, and objects that embody that purpose. Thus, the subtle patterns of activity and the outer shapes of matter are all created by a focus of purpose.

As we've discussed, when individual purpose is separate from the purpose and plan of the planetary life, the result is conflict within that life. However, when our purpose is aligned and at-one with that of the one life, the result is harmony within that life. Eventually each of us reaches a point—through long experience with opposition and conflict—where we realize that we must drop our inner conflict, at-one with the divine plan of the one life, and be part of that life.

At that point, we begin our quest for our purpose, place, and function within the planetary life.

Those who have already "found" their purpose may offer guidance, techniques, and other aid for your quest. However, you are the one who must "will to arise" and go to spirit.

> One can align with one's "own" spirit, and relate the purpose, power, and will of one's spirit with one's "own" problems.

> One can align with the spirit of a community, and relate the purpose, power and will of that community with the problems of that community.

> One can align with the spirit of humanity, and relate the purpose, power, and will of humanity with the problems of humanity

In each case, one begins by identifying as soul and aligning with spirit. The creative process remains the same, but the focus on the three aspects (spirit, consciousness, and matter) changes.

Take, for example the purpose of humanity. We know humanity has a purpose because it exists. Everything that exists, in order to exist, must consist of the two poles and the relationship between them. Everything is a synthesis of motivating spirit, relating consciousness, and creative matter. We have defined the motivation of spirit as purpose, power, and will, thus, since humanity exists within the one planetary life, we have a purpose within that life.

Aligning with, understanding, and at-oneing with that purpose can be difficult or simple. Which it appears to be depends entirely on you. One of the classic methods of arriving at our purpose is to compare humanity's life on Earth to a school where we are all students. When we complete our studies and graduate, we get to leave. The question then becomes, "what do human beings need to do, to achieve, in order to "graduate?"

There are many descriptions of this achievement. It has been called transcendence, enlightenment, and at-one-ment, among many others. But, the basic idea is this...

Human beings are "liberated" from the form when we become aware of our self as soul.

We "graduate" when we take the next step, and at-one as soul with the one planetary life.

Thus, it's all about the growth and development of the self or soul. We evolved from species awareness to individuality, and are now forcing ourselves to take the next step in evolution—planetary consciousness. What we are growing and developing is our consciousness, self, or soul.

The motivating purpose of humanity, within the planetary life, is the growth and development of consciousness.

Chapter 1

Everything we have done and everything we are doing is an expression of this purpose. Each of us, as a soul, is related to a portion of this purpose, and responsible for bringing that portion into appearance.

We immersed ourselves in matter for this purpose.

We developed a physical body, emotional instrument, and mental vehicle for this purpose.

We created all the chaos and crises of the world for this purpose.

We are arising from the form to spirit for this purpose.

We will explore this purpose further as we proceed, beginning with the following technique.

Aligning With Purpose in the Heart

While all of us create, most of us do so unconsciously. Learning to wield the Law of Relationship consciously, in service to the one planetary life, requires regular, persistent practice. The following is the first in a series of techniques designed to prepare the indwelling consciousness and persona instrument for conscious service. These preparatory inner exercises are followed by a series of service techniques that will help you take up your purpose, place, and function within the one life.

These preparatory techniques should be performed as described, in the sequence in which they appear. Prior inner work may be of assistance, but will not be a replacement if the intent behind them was different. Remember, the intent here is to help serve humanity by wielding the Law of Relationship. In order to prepare your consciousness and instrument for that, you must:

Identify as the soul within the one planetary life,

Align with a portion of the purpose of the one life,

Relate that motivating purpose to a condition within the world,

Observe the resulting creative activity of matter,

Relate that creative activity with its motivating purpose.

Inner work performed for another purpose may help the consciousness and instrument participate in this process.

Chapter 1

But, in order to perform it well they will still need to be practiced in this creative process *with the intent* to serve humanity.

The intent behind any inner technique focuses the consciousness and programs the persona. Thus, in the following exercises:

> The intent behind relaxing your physical body is to make it quiet, still, and receptive to the divine purpose conveyed to it by the soul.
>
> The intent behind calming and clarifying your emotions is to make your emotional instrument receptive and responsive to the divine purpose conveyed to it by the soul.
>
> The intent behind clarifying and focusing your mind is to make it receptive to the divine purpose conveyed to it by the soul.
>
> The intent behind integrating the body, emotions, and mind is to make the entire persona receptive and responsive to the divine purpose conveyed to it by the soul.

Thus, the motivating purpose behind the preparatory techniques is to prepare the indwelling consciousness and persona instrument for service to the planetary life. We will begin with a simple relaxation:

Aligning the Physical Instrument

Close your eyes and relax your physical body, beginning with your toes and moving upward to your head. You may command each portion to relax, imagine a soothing warmth or tingling sensation, or use whatever other method works for you.

Include every portion of your body, paying special attention to your tummy, diaphragm, heart, and neck. (Pause for a few moments.)

Slowly move your identity into your physical heart, and become aware that you, the conscious thinking "I" are now the soul in the heart. (Pause, and hold this awareness, for about a minute.)

As the soul in the heart, become aware that you are an integral part of the one planetary life. (Pause for about a minute.)

As the soul in the one life, aspire to know your purpose and function within that life. When that aspiration reaches its height, *audibly sound (say)* the *OM*.

Recognize that that call will draw your purpose into your life and affairs.

Take a deep breath, and slowly open your eyes.

If performed regularly, this technique will help align your physical instrument with the purpose of the planetary life. Upcoming techniques will build on the foundation of this one. Thus, we strongly recommend that you perform this alignment regularly, perhaps once a day, for at least one week.

The next step in the awakening process appears at the end of the following chapter, "Awakening Your Awareness."

Chapter 2

Awakening Your Awareness

Our self awareness or identity is also part of the Law of Relationship. Most human beings become aware of their self, as an individual, sometime around age two. From then on, when we look into a mirror we see our individual self. This is a normal stage in the development of humanity, and is the source of our ability to relate with others as individuals—"I am over here, you are over there".

However, whenever we create from a *self-centered identity* (*my* self, *my* family, *my* business, etc.), that identity is isolated from and out of harmony with the planetary life, and the results will be detrimental to that life. This is inevitable, because self awareness or identity is part of the Law and helps determine the effects of all creative activity.

Awakening and Expanding Your Identity

Sit comfortably with your back straight, your feet flat on the floor and your arms on the chairs armrests or in your lap.

Close your eyes and imagine a soothing warmth, a tingling sensation, golden light (or whatever other method works for you) beginning in your toes... and slowly moving into your feet... ankles... forelegs...knees... thighs... buttocks... tummy... lower back... diaphragm... upper

back... heart... fingers... hands... forearms... upper
arms... shoulders... neck... tongue... scalp...the muscles
of the face... and the muscles behind the eyes.

Move your self awareness into your heart. If it helps, you
may picture a tiny version of yourself standing within a
sphere of golden-white light in the middle of your chest.

From your position in the heart, imagine lines of light
moving out from you, linking you with every one and every
thing in the planetary life.

Become aware that you are part of that Life—that you exist within it.

When your awareness of that Life reaches its height, *audibly sound (say) the OM.*

Take a deep breath, and slowly open your eyes.

Chapter 2 Commentary

Part A

We are blessed to live at a time when the consequences of selfishness are inescapable. The air we breathe, the water we drink, the food we eat, and the earth we walk on—all have been and are being poisoned by our selfishness.

When we first become aware of this relationship between the separated soul and the destruction around us we tend to conclude that our separative identity must be bad or evil. As we grow further, we gradually recognize that every level of awareness, even separation, has its place in the planetary life.

There are many levels and states of identity, each of which has its particular place in and affects on the one life. In order to achieve its purpose (the growth and development of consciousness) the planetary life experiences and utilizes each of these stages and states of awareness. These levels and states of awareness may be described in many ways, including "internal" and "external".

Internal states of awareness are ours alone. They are part of our individual identity, and include all the levels of individual self awareness. While others experience identical stages of individual awareness, in each case that identity is unique to that individual.

External states of awareness are not ours alone, but are

shared with others. They are part of our larger identity within the one life, and of our relationship with that life. While we may experience these states from an individual perspective, each of these external states is actually a single awareness. They have many individualized points of expression, but they are shared by those many points rather than separate and unique.

States of Awareness

The "external" states of awareness include: species, individual, group, kingdom, and planetary consciousness.

Species Consciousness

The consciousness of a species is a single state of identity, a single "I am" within the one planetary life. That "I am" remains part of the planetary "I am," but with a quality unique to that species. That unique "I am" sounds within the entire species, and within every member of that species. Each and all of us share and experience the characteristic "I am" of the human species, and can recognize each other as "human" because of it. The "I am" of humanity sounds within each and all of us.

The same is true of every species within the one planetary life. Each has its self or soul, part of the one soul of the planetary life. That species soul sounds it's characteristic "I am" as a species, and thus within every member of that species.

However, because species consciousness precedes individual consciousness, it can be difficult for individualized human beings to understand, to separate from our individual awareness. The following story may help clarify what we mean:

> Once upon a time, an old widow purchased two parakeets, Chip and Chirp, to keep her company. She took great joy in their song, which relieved her loneliness, and took great care of Chip and Chirp. Eventually, however, Chip sickened and died, despite the widow's care, leaving Chirp alone. Chirp became listless and stopped singing. Seeing this, the widow placed a parakeet-size mirror in Chirp's cage. When Chirp gazed into the mirror, she saw a parakeet and began to sing again, for she was no longer lonely.

The "I am" sounding within Chirp was the "I am" of her species. Thus, when she gazed in the mirror she recognized that image as a parakeet. However, since parakeets have not yet achieved individual consciousness, Chirp did not recognize her self, for she had no individual self to recognize.

Individual Consciousness

Individual identity is also a single "I am" within the one planetary life. It is a refinement of the planetary "I am" that enables the self or soul to focus its identity or self as an individual within a species. That "I am" remains part of the species consciousness, which remains part of the planetary consciousness.

This and other refinements in the planetary "I am" can be compared to the ability of the human eye to focus at different distances.

Imagine that you are sitting in a chair on a sandy beach. It is a perfect, sunny day—warm, but not hot, a few fluffy clouds dot the sky, and a gentle breeze stirs the air. Seagulls call in the distance, waves crash, and children call to each other. A red and green beach umbrella provides an island of shade, and a colorful cotton towel keeps the sand away from your sunscreen-slathered body. The chair is one of those folding things whose legs are just long enough to keep your butt off the sand.

Now, gently touch your index finger to the warm sand, so that a single grain sticks to it. Hold the finger, pointed up, before your face, and focus on the single grain of sand on the tip of your finger. Note the color of the grain, its shape, texture, and size. Focus on nothing else but that grain of sand, until it becomes the entire focus of your world.

This singleness of focus is what creates individuality. Individual consciousness occurs when the planetary life focuses on and identifies with a "single grain of sand"— a tiny portion of itself. It remains the "I am" of the planetary life, but sounding within many minute portions of that life.

This differentiation of the One into the Many makes each and every portion of the One unique. Each and every minute portion of that one "I am" has its own unique qualities, a unique relationship with the planetary purpose, and a unique relationship with the planetary matter.

Thus, within humanity the "I am" of the planetary life has differentiated itself into a species, and within the

Chapter 2

human species into individual identities or souls. It is one planetary soul, differentiated by the refined ability to focus the "I am."

Within this planetary life, the human kingdom and species is unique in its ability, as a species, to focus and sound the "I am" as an individual. Thus, it is normal and natural for human beings to be self aware. Human beings normally attain individual awareness around age two, thus:

> When Billie was 18 months and three days old, he crawled into his parent's bedroom. There, he spotted movement in the mirrored surface of a closet door, crawled over to investigate, and discovered a baby. Billie was fascinated. He smiled and the baby smiled. He giggled, waved an arm, and the baby appeared to giggle and waved an arm. Billie played with the baby for some time, before losing interest and crawling away.

Billie did not recognize the image as himself because he did not yet have an individual "I am."

> When Tracy was 4 years old, her parents took her to the local county fair. At the fair, they visited a face-painting booth. Tracy watched wide-eyed as young children had their faces painted. When her turn came, a young artist asked her what she wanted, and Tracy asked for butterflies. As she sat in her mother's lap, the artist painted bright butterflies on Tracy's face—red and yellow on her right cheek, and blue and orange on her left. When the artist was done, she held up a mirror so Tracy could see. Tracy gazed at her image in the mirror, touched her right cheek, and laughed in delight.

Tracy recognized the painted image as herself because she had an individual "I am," an individual self.

While individual awareness is normal for human beings, it is also beginning to develop in a few members of other species, such as great apes and elephants, and perhaps dogs, dolphins, and others.

As the consciousness and personality of an individual evolves, they pass through many stages of individual awareness, identifying first as their physical appetites, and later as their emotional feelings and thoughts. Finally, however, after many long ages of experience, we begin to realize that we are not our body, emotions, or mind, but that we are the "I am," the soul, that has identified with and lost itself within the persona.

We then begin to seek release from the "prison" of the persona via identification with and as our true self. This quest is sometimes called the "path of liberation," and is typified by the effort to escape the worlds of the persona by rising above them.

Many of the world's spiritual traditions include some expression of the path of liberation. It is a normal and natural part of the growth and development of the soul, but it has its own difficulties, which include:

> The individual on the path of liberation is often more self involved, and unconsciously separative, than is the individual identified with their persona. This occurs because of the growing focus on the higher self or soul, accompanied by an attempt to withdraw from the persona nature. The initial result is usually a period of detachment, experienced as disinterest or

44

even repulsion, from the everyday physical, emotional, and mental life of humanity.

Depending on how they approach and experience the path of liberation, individuals on it experience some or all of the persona instrument as impediments or obstacles to liberation. For instance, those using the mystical path or method of blissful union, tend to see the intellect as an obstacle. Those on the occult path of liberation through knowledge tend to view the emotions as an obstacle, and on either path seekers tend to view the physical body as an obstacle. The result of this attitude toward the persona instrument is a misrelationship with that instrument. This misrelationship must be transformed before one can utilize the instrument in service to the planetary life.

Many attempt to consciously apply the Law of Relationship to their self liberation. However, since the conscious creative process uses the mind, emotions, bio-electric, and physical bodies, we cannot wield the Law effectively so long as we have a misrelationship with any portion of that instrument.

Remember, because of the way the Law works, our persona instrument will respond to whatever intent we focus upon it.

So long as we identify the physical and bio-electric bodies as obstacles to growth, they will believe us, resist our growth, and pull us back from the life of the soul into our worldly affairs.

So long as we identify the emotional feeling nature as an obstacle to our growth, it will believe us and resist our liberation. Our emotions will respond to every attempt to rise above them by pulling us back down into their depths.

So long as we identify the mental nature as an obstacle to liberation, it will believe us. Our mechanism of thought will resist our attempts to achieve liberation by pulling us back into the realm of the mind.

We move past this resistance as we realize that matter, including that of our persona instrument, is as much a part of the one planetary life as is the soul. We then transform our relationship with matter by impressing a new purpose upon it—that part of the planetary purpose with which we, as soul, are related and for which we are responsible. That matter then becomes a functioning part of the body of the one life.

As the persona is impressed with this new intent it transforms into a vehicle for the indwelling soul, and the soul is able to realize its self through that vehicle. The self then becomes the awakened soul in the world.

As the obstacles to self awareness drop away, one realizes that the soul is aware of itself on a number of levels. The first of these is sometimes called group consciousness.

Chapter 2 Commentary

Part B

Group Consciousness

The soul's levels of self awareness are really fields of focus. Continuing the analogy of human sight, we might say that so long as we remain identified with and as our individual self, the focus of our self is very "near sighted"—limited to that of our individual consciousness. However, as we awaken to the soul our focal range expands beyond our immediate self identity to include ever broader vistas of consciousness. These broader vistas or levels of soul awareness include the "I am" of groups, kingdoms, and the entire planetary life.

Each of these levels of soul awareness is formulated by the Law of Relationship, and thus can be distinguished by the three aspects of that Law—Purpose, Consciousness, and Matter.

As we become aware of and as the soul, we begin to realize that, as the soul we have a purpose within the one planetary life. That purpose is not ours alone, but is a shared group purpose.

> Use your creative imagination to return to the beach. Recall the sky, sunlight, clouds, waves, breeze, seagulls, children, umbrella, towel, chair, and sand.

> Now, dip your hand into the warm sand, cupping a

small handful containing thousands of grains. Hold your cupped hand before your face, and focus on the thousands of grains of sand. Note the color and texture of the mound, and feel its warmth.

Focus on nothing else but that mound of sand, until it becomes the entire focus of your world.

Hold that focus for a few moments, and then relax your attention.

This singleness of focus is what creates a group consciousness or identity. Group consciousness occurs when the planetary life focuses on and identifies with a "mound of sand"—a tiny portion of itself that includes many individual grains or identities. It remains the "I am" of the planetary life, but sounding within a tiny portion of that life.

This is comparable to the purpose of the cells in the pulse point of the human heart. The function of the heart as a whole is to circulate the life energy of the bodies (in the physical body, that life energy is carried in the blood). All the cells in the physical heart share that purpose, but portions of the heart specialize in portions of that purpose.

For instance, a valve may be responsible for allowing blood into the heart, while another lets the blood out. One group of cells may be responsible for initiating a pulse, while another is responsible for stopping it. In each case, all the cells within that portion of the heart—valve, pulse point, or whatever—share the same purpose.

This shared purpose, placement, and function is another

Chapter 2

The group as a whole is responsible for any and all patterns of negativity that exist within the group persona. If an individual persona within the group has a misrelationship with money and finance, then that negative pattern exists within the group persona and will affect the entire persona. Every portion of the group will be affected by that pattern to some extent, and the entire group, individually and collectively, are response-able for it. That response-ability includes transforming that negative pattern by relating that condition (misrelationship with money) with the overshadowing portion of the planetary purpose, and that overshadowing purpose with that embodied group condition. It is a simple application of the Law of Relationship, but it must be performed before the group is able to take up its purpose, place, and function within humanity.

Transforming the patterns of negativity within its persona is part of the training of a group. As we transform those patterns, we transform our group persona, and the individual personas within it, into a vehicle of the soul.

The group as a whole is also responsible for a portion of the planetary purpose or plan. Whenever the group encounters a pattern of negativity that opposes the group purpose, the group is response-able for transforming it. The group relates that negative condition with the overshadowing purpose, and that overshadowing purpose with that embodied condition. The matter of that negative condition responds to that new focus of motivating purpose by changing its movement, by taking on a new shape and form. The result is a positive pattern and a new condition within the realms of thought and feeling, and the material world. It is a simple application of the Law of Relationship, but this is how a group soul performs its function within the planetary life.

By the regular, persistent practice of the Law in this way, the group soul gradually takes up its purpose, place, and function within the planetary life. As the group does so, the focal range of the group soul expands, until eventually it expands beyond that of the group "I am" to include even broader states of awareness.

Kingdom (Humanity) Consciousness

The identity of our kingdom, humanity, is also a single "I am" within the one planetary life. That single "I am" of humanity is part of the identity of every human being, at every level of growth and development. Or, perhaps more accurately, the soul of every human being exists within and is part of the soul of humanity. Thus, no matter how evolved the consciousness, or how refined our focus of awareness, we all share this identity.

> When we think, "I am a human being," that is the "I am" of humanity sounding within our mind.

> When we feel, "I am a human being," that is the "I am" of humanity sounding within our emotions.

> When we sense, "I am a human being," that is the "I am" of humanity sounding within our bio-electrical and physical bodies.

However, while the "I am" of humanity exists within every portion of humanity, our experience of that "I am" changes as we evolve. As we refine our focus of awareness, this collective "I am" becomes clearer.

This refinement of the planetary "I am" can be compared

to an expansion of the ability of the human eye to focus at different distances:

> Again, use your creative imagination to return to the beach. Recall the sky, sunlight, clouds, waves, breeze, seagulls, children, umbrella, towel, chair, and a handful of sand.

> Keeping your palm up and your gaze fixed on the mound of sand, slowly turn, and slide your hand into the warm sand.

> Recognize that, although it has returned to the beach, the mound of sand remains in your consciousness.

> Now, slowly lift your gaze from your hand to the beach, and focus on the vast reaches of sand before you. Note the color and texture of the beach, and feel its texture and warmth.

> Focus on nothing else but that beach, until it becomes the entire focus of your world.

> Hold that focus for a few moments, and then relax your attention.

This singleness of focus is what reunites us with the consciousness of our kingdom. It occurs when the planetary life focuses on and identifies with an "entire beach"—a vast portion of the planetary life that includes myriads of individual grains and many group mounds.

We do the same thing when we identify as the human kingdom. That kingdom has its own identity, part of the "I am" of the planetary life. As we refine our focus of awareness, we increase the range, detail, and flexibility of our focus of identity:

> Our range expands to include every state of awareness from species, through individuality and group, to that of our kingdom, and beyond.

> Our detail increases, enabling us to identify with the fragments of identity within an individual personality.

> Our flexibility grows, enabling us to identify as any portion of the larger group of which we are a part.

The result of this is that we can wield the Law of Relationship as any portion of the one planetary life. We can identify as our individual self, and use the creative process to transform any portion of that self.

We can identify as our group or kingdom, and, as that group or kingdom, use the creative process to transform that group or kingdom.

We can do this in right relationship because we are performing the creative process *as* that which is being transformed. We are, in each case, transforming our self by bringing our purpose (individual, group, or kingdom) into right relationship with our matter.

> This can be illustrated by revisiting our beach analogy:

> Again, using your creative imagination, return to the scene at the beach, and recall the sky, sunlight, clouds, waves, breeze, seagulls, children, umbrella, towel, chair, and handful of sand. Recall holding the mound of sand cupped in your hand. Keeping your palm up and your gaze fixed on the mound of sand,

slowly lift your other hand and touch your index finger to the mound, so that the tip of your finger is covered in sand.

Turn the tip of your index finger upright, and hold it before your face.

Note the color and texture of the sand covering your finger.

Focus on nothing else but that finger tip of sand, until it becomes the entire focus of your world.

Hold that focus for a few moments, and then move the finger back over the mound and rub your finger against your thumb so that the sand on the finger drops back onto the mound.

Slowly relax your attention.

Just as the human eye can focus on an individual grain of sand, the entire scene, or anything in between, once we achieve group awareness, we can focus on and identify as any portion of that group. We can be aware of or identify as an individual, our group, our kingdom, or anything in between.

In addition, when we become aware of a thought, feeling, or pattern of behavior, we can see the place of that thought, feeling, or behavior within the larger life. We can see its purpose, its relationships, and its effects, whether it is an accurate expression or a distortion of divine intent, and we have a means (via the Law of Relationship) to transform any distortions.

This includes our own, individual thoughts, feelings,

and behaviors. The awakened consciousness experiences them as part of the persona of the greater life. Thus, when one transforms patterns within one's individual persona, one transforms those patterns within the greater life.

By the regular, persistent practice of the Law in this way, individual souls gradually take up their purpose, place, and function within humanity.

As individual human souls take up their function, the focal range of their identity grows beyond that of their present "I am" to include ever broader states of awareness. Eventually, the "I am" of every human being will grow to include species ("I am human"), individual ("I am an individual"), and soul ("I am soul") consciousness.

At that point, whenever a human looks in a mirror or at another person they will see:

A member of their species,

An individual human being, and

A fellow soul.

Since the soul is aware of relationships, once we are aware of ourselves and each other as soul we will automatically see our relationships rather than our differences. This will change every aspect of our life and affairs.

Chapter 2 Commentary

Part C

Planetary Consciousness

The soul of Earth is the "I am" within which we live, and move, and have our being. Every kingdom, species, group, and individual identity is a focus of that one planetary "I am."

The soul of humanity exists within and is part of the soul of Earth. Within that one soul, every part of the planetary life—no matter how large or how small—is related with every other part. Thus, no matter how evolved the consciousness or refined the focus of awareness, every soul shares this one identity.

Awareness of that oneness is temporarily lost or veiled when it identifies as portions of itself, such as kingdoms. The unique quality and character of that kingdom differentiates it from the rest of the planetary life, and enables it to discover its purpose, place, and function within the greater life.

Similarly, our awareness of the consciousness of the human kingdom is temporarily obscured when that kingdom identifies as portions of itself. The unique quality and character of the resulting individual souls differentiates each soul from the others, and gives each a purpose, place, and function within the human kingdom.

As we complete our individual growth and development,

we realize that we are not our thoughts, our emotions, or our bodies, but that we are a soul within the one life. We realize that, as soul, we have a purpose and function within that life. We realize that we are part of the soul of humanity, and of Earth.

With that realization comes responsibility. Our increased awareness of relationship—as a part with the whole, and of the whole with its parts—expands our ability to relate. Our increased ability to relate expands our ability to perform the Magic of Consciousness.

> Again, use your creative imagination to return to the beach. Recall the sky, sunlight, clouds, waves, breeze, seagulls, children, umbrella, towel, chair, and sand.
>
> Place a hand on the sand, palm down, and feel its texture and warmth.
>
> Listen to the calls of gulls, the crash of waves, and the glad cries of children.
>
> Gaze at the sand near your hand, and then lift your gaze to include the entire beach, the waves and ocean beyond, and the sky.
>
> Recognize that everything in this scene—the sand, people, gulls, water, and air, is part of the one planetary life.
>
> Focus on everything in the scene at once, until it becomes the entire focus of your world.
>
> Retaining your awareness of the whole, slowly contract your focus back to the beach, within the beach

to the mound of sand, and within the mound to a single grain.

Hold that focus for a few moments, and then relax your attention.

When we learn to focus on "our" soul, we learn to focus as soul. Once we can focus as soul, we can focus as any soul within the planetary life. We learn to see the self or soul in anyone and everyone.

As the soul, we can wield the Law of Relationship, relating the purpose overshadowing a soul with the matter outpicturing it, and with the matter overshadowing it, bringing the purpose and matter into union or at-one-ment. This is the basis of our work within the one life. It is how Earth will awaken from the long dark night of the soul and emerge into divine light.

* * *

In order to achieve its purpose (the growth and development of consciousness) the planetary life experiences and utilizes each of these states of awareness.

Each of the above states of awareness has a spectrum or range. The more developed the consciousness of a kingdom, species, or individual, the greater the range of awareness. The range of a kingdom grows and develops as the range of its parts grow and develop. Thus, as we evolve as individual souls, the soul of humanity grows and evolves.

Like the spectrum of light, that range can be divided into types and levels, each of which has its own qualities and characteristics. For instance:

How to Serve Humanity

There are thousands of species in the animal kingdom, each with its own particular quality of consciousness, and each with its own typical level of awareness.

The consciousness of a clam is quite dim and undeveloped, and the range of the species consciousness is quite narrow. The consciousness of one species of clam is quite similar to that of another.

The consciousness of a bird species is much more advanced than that of a clam, and the range of consciousness between bird species is much greater than that between clam species.

The consciousness of the canine species is more advanced than that of birds, and the range of canine consciousness is much broader. More advanced dogs even show signs of dawning self awareness.

The consciousness of the human species is more advanced than that of any of the so-called "lower" kingdoms, and the range of human consciousness is also much broader. That range includes everything from species through individual self-awareness. Within that individual consciousness are a variety of levels of awareness. These levels of awareness encompass the entire "I am" spectrum of individual human beings.

Levels of Individual Awareness

Humanity has an ongoing role in the evolution of the planetary consciousness or soul. As a kingdom within that life, we have attained a variety of such states already. As individuals within the human kingdom, we experience each of the human states of awareness, and the expression of those states via the Law of Relationship. The major states of human awareness, and their consequences within the Law, include:

"I am my physical body."

Many members of humanity are so identified with their physical bodies that they examine their life and affairs in terms of physical achievements or conditions. This may include: "I am fat", "I am thin", "I am pretty," "I am bald," etc.

We were "trapped" within this state of awareness when we first moved into and identified as our physical bodies. When we identified as the body, rather than the soul, we forgot our self and took on the abilities and limits of the form. This focused our creative efforts on perfecting our body, rather than the soul. If "I am my body," then when I strengthen my body, I strengthen my self. If I neglect or fall prey to the appetites of my body, then I neglect my self.

Thus, our identification as the physical body compelled us to develop or "perfect" that body much more rapidly and with greater refinement than we might have otherwise. Those members of humanity who aspired to something beyond their current state (and who does not) responded by developing physical disciplines designed to "perfect" the physical instrument—strengthen it, increase its flexibility and sensitivity, etc. Descendants of these disciplines are still with us today, in such practices as the asanas or postures of hatha yoga, and can be quite beneficial if used with right intent.

The true purpose of the physical instrument is found

within the planetary purpose. From this perspective, the purpose of the physical body is to be a vehicle of the soul—a vehicle through which the soul can grow and develop, and with which the soul can perform its function within the planetary life.

The physical instrument of humanity has advanced considerably, and is now much more sensitive and flexible than ever before. However, that advancement was gained at considerable cost. Once we were "trapped" in the separated form, we remained there throughout the process of developing a fit vehicle (body, emotions, and mind). And, the pattern of learning through separation, and the chaos and destruction of separation, became the primary learning method of humanity.

This process of learning through negativity has been normal for humanity for many long ages, but it is not natural and has had considerable effect on our spiritual paths. For instance, aspiration to union or at-one-ment with the one life is often preceded by the desire to escape the "prison of form."

This desire to escape form produced a misrelationship with matter that persists to this day. As mentioned above, depending on the tradition (and one's dwelling place in the body), the various levels of matter were seen as obstacles to union, rather than as aids to it. Thus, many seekers sought to suppress and escape the body, emotions, or mind. This desire to escape crippled their ability to work with that portion of the vehicle.

Remember, matter responds to the intent related to it by the consciousness. If you believe that physical form is an obstacle, and that your goal is to escape from the physical realm, your body will believe you! It will respond to that motivating purpose by being an obstacle. This is how the Law of Relationship works!

All types and levels of matter within the one planetary life are part of that life. A portion of that matter appears separate when the individual self identifies it as separate. The individual then focuses "their" will on "their" form. That "separated" form then behaves like a parasite, as if it lives within but is not part of the planetary life. This parasitic behavior of the physical form is entirely due to our individual self awareness.

As long as we are identified as isolated individuals, the forms we create (wielding the Law of Relationship) relate with the planetary life as though they are not part of that life.

- Their purpose is part of the purpose of the separated self that created them.

- Their consciousness is part of the separated self that created them.

- Their matter is part of the matter of the separated self that created them.

Everything humanity has created as the separated self is poisoned in this way. This is, essentially, a problem of right relationship. It is the normal and natural function of the soul to relate purpose with matter and matter with purpose.

- To the extent that soul is identified with and as the soul of the planetary life, then it relates the planetary purpose with planetary matter.

- To the extent that soul is identified with and as an individual self, then it relates "its" individual purpose with "its" matter.

Over the ages, humanity has created myriads of forms that are programmed with the separate, selfish purpose of individuals, families, communities, and nations. The result is a huge reservoir of separated forms, toxic to the larger life, that are part of the thought, feeling, and physical nature of humanity. This includes the forms of government, education, business, banking and finance, organization, art, science, religion, and every other sector of the old civilization. The only way to transform these separated forms is to awaken to our identity within the planetary life, and relate our separated forms with the planetary purpose.

When we relate our physical matter to the planetary purpose, our physical forms will take their proper place and function within the planetary life. They will become instruments of the soul, and part of the body of the planetary life.

Our physical bodies will become radiant sources of divine light within the one planetary life.

"I am my body electric."

We attained this additional state of awareness when we first moved into and identified as our bio-electrical energy field or vital body. This complex energy field is the underlying structure or framework around which the physical body is built. In fact, the physical body is actually

Chapter 2

a reflection or condensation of the bio-electrical body.[2]

As we developed our physical instrument, it gradually increased its sensitivity to the bio-electrical. As we sensed that body, we turned our attention to, identified with, and became trapped within it. We took on the abilities, and limitations, of the bio-electrical body.

This expanded the focus of our creative efforts beyond perfecting the physical to include perfecting our bio-electrical instrument, and integrating that instrument with the physical body.

Today, the integration between our physical and electrical bodies is so complete that the two are usually experienced as a single state of consciousness and as a single body—the physical-electric.

As before, our identification as the physical-electric compelled us to develop or "perfect" that body much more rapidly and with greater refinement than we might have otherwise.

This may be compared to the relative progress of an amateur tennis player and a professional. In this case, their motivations are quite different. The amateur plays occasionally, for recreational pleasure, and has a relatively small attachment to or investment in the game. The professional practices daily, for their survival, and has a much greater attachment to or investment in the game.

Again, those members of humanity who aspired to grow

---

[2] There are many names for this bio-electrical energy, including: "chi," "prana," and "physical-etheric."

and develop (and who does not) responded by developing outer physical and inner electrical practices designed to "perfect" the physical-electric instrument—purify it, increase its intensity, raise its frequency, and direct it at will. Descendants of these disciplines are with us today, in such practices as qigong, tai chi chuan, and pranayama, and can be quite beneficial if used with right intent.

The true purpose of the physical-electric instrument is found within the planetary purpose. From this perspective, the purpose of the physical-electric is to be the true physical vehicle of the Soul—a vehicle through which the soul can grow and develop, and with which the soul can perform its function within the planetary life.

The physical-electric instrument of humanity has advanced considerably, and is now much more integrated and sensitive. However, it is not as powerful as in the distant past, as it is no longer the primary focus of our growth and development. The soul of humanity has moved on, to identify with additional portions of the instrument. We are now very aware of and identified as the emotional instrument, and growing into the mental.

"I am my emotions."

We attained this additional state of awareness as we moved into and identified as our emotional feeling nature. This complex body is the underlying structure that processes the force of emotions, within our environment and within our persona.

As we developed the emotional nature, we identified with and became trapped within our emotional feelings.

Chapter 2

We took on the abilities, and limitations, of the emotional body.

This expanded the focus of our creative efforts beyond perfecting the physical and bio-electrical, to include perfecting our emotions and using the force of our emotions (and of the portion of the planetary life under our influence) to control our physical and bio-electrical bodies and environment.

Emotions are the predominant identity of most modern human beings—"I am angry," "I am happy," "I am in love," "I wish you hadn't done that," etc. So long as the emotional identity is predominant, it directs and controls the rest of the persona. Thus, so long as our emotions are predominant:

- Our mind processes thoughts, accepting and rejecting them, according to how we *feel* about them. We do not truly "think," but opinionate. For instance, how you feel about taxes, education, reproduction, or military service will mold your thoughts on those subjects.

- Our bio-electrical body processes energy, directing its flow according to how we *feel* about that energy. For instance, how you feel about money molds the flow of economic energy within your bio-electrical body. This in turn has a direct affect on your outer abundance or lack.

- Our physical body acts, moving within the world according to how we *feel* about those activities. For instance, how you feel about a physical activity has a direct affect on the strength of your

body. An activity that you enjoy strengthens the
body, while an activity you dislike weakens it.

Thus, for emotionally identified members of humanity
our emotions are our motives. Our purpose in life, the
power to be in the world, are appropriated and directed
by our individual feelings. Our separate identity isolates
the force of our emotions from the force of the planetary
life, and the result is harmful to that life.

As always, the true purpose of the emotional instrument
is found within the planetary purpose. From this perspective, the purpose of the emotional feeling nature is
to be part of the vehicle of the Soul—a vehicle that relates thoughts within the one life to the bio-electrical
activity of that life, helping create the appearance of the
planetary life in the world of affairs. The emotions become an instrument through which the soul can grow
and develop, and with which the soul can perform its
function within the planetary life.

As with the physical and bio-electrical, our identification as our emotions compelled us to develop or "perfect"
that body much more rapidly and with greater refinement than we might have otherwise.

Humanity responded by developing inner practices designed to "perfect" the emotional instrument—purify it,
raise its frequency and intensity, and direct it at will.
Descendants of these disciplines are with us today, in
such practices as visualization and mysticism.

The chaos and destruction of our separated emotions
forces us to learn to control them, and eventually leads
us to aspire to union with the greater life of which we

are a part. This is the mystical path of joy, bliss, and at-one-ment. For emotional humanity, the mystical path was the primary method of spiritual growth and development, but today it is more often part of the preparation for the path of service to the planetary life.

Purifying and directing the emotions remains a necessity (part of the preparation for performing the creative process), but it is often neglected by more mentally focused members of humanity.

"I am my thoughts."

Growing portions of humanity are aspiring to a mentally focused life. They idolize the ability to think clearly and rationally, to formulate a complex plan of action, to solve a mystery, etc. Via that aspiration, we are developing a mental instrument that can sense, formulate, and direct thought. However, at this point most of us do not yet truly live in our mind.

We began attaining this additional state of awareness as we developed, moved into, and identified as our mental nature. This complex body is the underlying structure that processes the energy of thoughts, within our environment and within our persona.

As we develop the mental nature, we identify with and become trapped within our thoughts. We take on the abilities, and limitations, of the mental body, including its ability to organize and its difficulty in relating.

The mental body is expanding the focus of our creative efforts beyond perfecting the physical, bio-electrical, and emotional to include perfecting our mind and using the energy of thought (and of the portion of the planetary life under our influence) to control our physical, bio-electrical, and emotional bodies and environment.

Humanity is presently transitioning from an emotional identity, "I am my feelings," to a mental identity "I am my thoughts." During much of this transition period our emotions are still the predominant identity, and so long as this is the case our feelings direct and control our thoughts. Rather than thinking first, and using our emotions to empower our thoughts, we feel first and our emotions control our thoughts. We see some of the effects of this every day, when otherwise intelligent people have completely irrational opinions about something they are emotionally identified with. For instance, we often see examples of this in political and religious views; particularly when the two are combined.

So long as we are identified with and captivated by that emotional identification (with "our" team, "our" political party, "our" religion, "our" nation, etc.) our emotions wield the Law of Relationship and create our lives:

- That feeling directs and controls our thoughts.

- Our bio-electrical body is empowered by the force of our emotions.

- Our physical body acts, moving within the world according to our opinions.

Gradually, via the long painful path of experience, we force ourselves to develop the mind to the point where our intellect can control our emotions, at first by suppressing them.

Chapter 2

When we suppress our emotions unconsciously, we "take the wind from our sails," and lack the force to create. When we suppress our emotions consciously, we have finer control, but the effect is the same. Both unconscious and conscious suppression give us a reprieve from our feelings, but only for as long as we can keep a lid on them. Eventually, our suppressed feelings will find a way to express themselves, spraying their force into our bodies and environment. This outpictures in our lives as sudden explosions of emotional force—including everything from shouting and physical violence to high-pitched, barking laughter.

For mentally identified members of humanity our thoughts are our motives. Our purpose in life, the power to be in the world, is appropriated and directed by our individual thoughts. Our separate identity isolates the energy of our thoughts from the energy of the planetary life, and the result is harmful to that life.

As always, the true purpose of the mental instrument is found within the planetary purpose. From this perspective, the purpose of the mental nature is to be part of the vehicle of the Soul—a vehicle that formulates thoughts, and organizes thoughts into plans of action within the one life. Our thoughts become an instrument through which the soul can grow and develop, and with which the soul can perform its function within the planetary life.

As with the physical, bio-electrical, and emotional, our identification as our thoughts (Descartes' "I think, therefore I am.") compelled us to develop or "perfect" that body much more rapidly and with greater refinement than we might have otherwise.[3]

Humanity responded by developing inner practices designed to "perfect" the mental instrument—gather mental matter, focus it, and direct it at will. Descendants of these disciplines are with us today, in such practices as calculation, reason, and contemplation.

The chaos and destruction of our separated thoughts force us to learn to control them, and eventually leads us to aspire to union with the greater life of which we are a part. This is the path of knowledge. For rational humanity, the path of knowledge is the primary method of spiritual growth and development, but today it is more and more often part of the preparation for the path of service to the planetary life.

Focusing and directing our thoughts remains a necessity (part of the preparation for performing the creative process), but the necessary disciplines are often neglected by more mentally focused members of humanity.

"I am my persona."

We attain this additional state of awareness when we integrate our body, emotions, and mind into a single, coherent unit. Up to this point, each of our bodies has its own motivating purpose and resulting activity. At any given moment, the purpose of the mind may or may not be compatible with that of the emotional body, and that of the emotional body may or may not be compatible with that of the physical-electric. For instance, we

---

[3] Descartes got it wrong. It's actually "'I' am therefore I am." The "I" is the proof of existence. Thought is merely a vehicle for the "I."

may know that we need to control our diet, but have an intense desire for cheesecake. Due to the Law of Relationship, the conflict between the motives must eventually produce conflict in our life and affairs.

However, as before, that conflict forces us to grow—it is the means we have chosen for evolution. As we continue to develop our physical-electric, emotional, and mental bodies, the conflict grows in intensity. Eventually, that conflict forces us to integrate our persona into a single, coherent unit. When this is achieved:

- There is one motivating purpose for the entire persona. This single purpose is much more focused, powerful, and effective than the earlier conflicting purposes.

- There is one identity of the entire persona. The "I" of the persona includes the "I" of the physical-electric, the "I" of the emotional, and the "I" of the mental. This single identity is much more magnetic (both attractive and radiatory) than the earlier conflicting identities.

- There is one body of matter for the entire persona. The physical-electric, emotional, and mental function as a single unit rather than as three. This single unit is much more effective than the earlier conflicting bodies.

This is a tremendous stage in self development, but it is still very separative and even more destructive.

- The motivating purpose of the persona is separate from the motivating purpose of the planetary life, and thus is toxic to that life.

- The consciousness of the persona is separate from the self or soul of the planetary life, and thus is destructive of that life.

- The matter of the persona appears separate from the matter of the planetary life, and thus behaves like a parasite within that life.

As always, the true purpose of the persona is found within the planetary purpose. From this perspective, the purpose of the persona is to be the vehicle of the Soul—a vehicle that transforms spirit into thought, feeling, and activity in the world of affairs. Through trial and experience, we slowly transform the persona into an instrument through which the soul can grow and develop, and with which the soul can perform its function within the planetary life.

As with the physical and bio-electrical, our identification as our persona compels us to develop or "perfect" that instrument much more rapidly and with greater refinement than we might have otherwise.

Humanity is developing a variety of inner practices designed to "perfect" the persona—integrate it, and align it with and make it receptive to the Soul. Disciplines that accomplish this include Integral Yoga and Kriya Yoga.

The chaos and destruction of our separated persona eventually forces us to turn our attention beyond our separate self, to the soul, to aspire to the soul, and identify with and as the individualized consciousness within the planetary life.

Chapter 2

"I am the soul."

We attain this additional state of awareness when, after long experience of the persona, we turn our attention inward and upward and aspire to know our true self. If you have asked yourself, "Who am I and why am I here?" then you have achieved this point of transition. In the following pages you will find techniques that will enable you to answer the question of "who" and "why", and, having found the answer, to take up your purpose, place, and function within the one life.

As we awaken to our true self, the emphasis of our inner work changes from relaxing the physical instrument, calming the emotions, and focusing the mind (although those are still included) to:

- Aligning our persona with our soul, and through our soul with the soul of the planetary life. The persona then becomes receptive to the magnetic impulse of the soul (both radiatory and attractive).

- Standing receptive to the purpose, power, and will of the soul, and through the soul with the purpose of the one life. The persona then merges its will with the will of soul, and all of our creative activities become expressions of the purpose, power, and will of the planetary life.

- Precipitating the will of the soul into appearance in the realms of the persona. Via the creative process, we shape that will into thought within the realm of mind, feeling in the realm of emotions, activity in the bio-electric realm, and appearance in the physical world.

How to Serve Humanity

This is the essence of the creative process, the Law of Relationship in action, as practiced by a light worker — one who works with and within the light of the soul. We will examine this process in greater detail, and perform it in service to the planetary life, as we proceed.

In the meantime, an essential preliminary step is that of dedication. Before the persona can become a vehicle for the soul, we must consecrate it to that purpose. This can be accomplished via any simple ritual that expresses the intent (to dedicate the persona to the soul) in words. The following is a simple example:

> Go to a quiet, secluded, outdoor location with no one else around. Standing in that place, gaze up at the sky and aspire to be at-one with the planetary life. When that aspiration reaches its height, audibly state:
>
> > *"I dedicate my persona to the soul, and through the soul to the one life of which I am an integral part."*
>
> Quietly hold that aspiration to and alignment with the soul for about three minutes.
>
> Audibly sound the *OM*.
>
> Gradually relax your attention and return to your normal awareness.

This exercise, or one like it, may be performed as often as you wish. When you do so, the dedication statement should be said only once, and not repeated.

Having made such dedication, your soul will create an opportunity to put it into action. There will inevitably be some conflict between the will of your persona and the will of the soul, as the persona strives to maintain its accustomed independence. However, if you persist in your dedication, and in expressing that dedication in your life and affairs, then the intent of your separate persona will gradually merge with that of the soul, and all such conflicts will cease.

How to Serve Humanity

Chapter 3

Awakening Your Personality

Our inner and outer activity is also part of the Law of Relationship. Most human beings develop sophisticated emotional, and mental abilities, as well as physical. This is normal and natural, and the source of our ability to focus and empower our outer activity.

However, whenever our creative activity is motivated by self interest and directed by a separative identity that activity is out of harmony with the planetary life and the results will be detrimental to that life. This is inevitable because activity is part of the Law and helps determine the effects of the Law.

Awakening and Aligning
Your Personality

Sit comfortably, close your eyes, and relax your physical body.

Move your self awareness into your heart.

Calm your emotions by picturing them as a perfectly calm, clear pool of water in a forest glade.

Listen to the sounds of the forest. What do you hear?

Become aware of the variety of odors. What do you smell?

Gaze into the mirror-smooth pool and see there the reflection of the deep-blue sky.

Take a deep breath, and as you slowly release it recognize that you physical body is part of the planetary life.

Take another deep breath, and as you slowly release it recognize that your emotions are part of the planetary life.

Take another deep breath, and as you slowly release it recognize that your thoughts are part of the planetary life.

Take another deep breath, and as you slowly release it recognize that your entire persona is part of the planetary life.

Align your persona—body, emotions, and mind—with the planetary life by audibly sounding the OM.

Take a deep breath, and slowly open your eyes.

Chapter 3 Commentary

We are blessed to live at a time of change, when we can transform the dark prison of the soul into a workshop of light.

Whether that transformation is simple or complex depends on us, on how we use of the Law of Relationship.

Our purpose can unify or isolate.

Our consciousness can at-one or divide.

Our matter can include or separate.

Everything that exists in the one life is formulated of these three, and each of these three can be aligned with or separated from the one life. Whether they are aligned or separated depends not on any one of them, but on all three.

> If our motivating purpose is isolated from that of the one life, then our consciousness and matter will be out of alignment with that life.
>
> If our relating consciousness identifies our self as separate from the one life, then our purpose and matter will be isolated from that life.
>
> If our matter is motivated by isolated purpose and separated self, then its activity will be out of harmony with the one life.

Since purpose, consciousness, and matter are three aspects of one life, whatever affects any one of them affects all three. Thus, transforming the persona from a "prison" into a vehicle of light includes working with all three. This is the creative process, the conscious use of the Law of Relationship.

When wielding the Law consciously, one keeps in mind the primary characteristics of each of the three:

Purpose motivates,

Consciousness relates, and

Matter differentiates.

This characteristic of matter enables the consciousness to evolve. As stated in chapter 2: "This differentiation of the One into the Many makes each and every portion of the One unique. Each and every minute portion of that one 'I am' has its own unique qualities, a unique relationship with the planetary purpose, and a unique relationship with the planetary matter.

"Thus, within humanity the 'I am' of the planetary life has differentiated itself into a species, and within the human species into individual identities or souls. It is one planetary soul, identified as many, and differentiated by matter."

The planetary soul is able to refine its focus because matter differentiates itself into many forms. Since everything that exists is a formulation of purpose, consciousness, and matter, whenever substance creates a new thought, a new feeling, or a new form there must be a purpose for and consciousness of that form. In the very act of identifying with that matter—that new thought, feeling, or form—consciousness refines its focus. Of course, the reverse is equally true. As consciousness focuses a new intent on matter, that matter responds by differentiating itself—by transforming or creating a new idea, feeling, or form. Thus, consciousness and matter evolve together.

This characteristic of matter is a crucial part of the Law of Relationship, for it helps us understand why our identity is so important. Matter naturally and normally differentiates—simplicity into complexity, one thing into many things, crude into refined. This is the process that drives the evolution of forms; forms that can express or imprison the soul, depending on the motivating identity within that form.

As we've discussed, our motivating purpose is determined by our identity.

If our "I am" is that of the larger life of which we are a part, then we align with and are motivated by the purpose of that larger life. Our identity and our purpose are inclusive. However, at this point the "I am" is farsighted—focused on the grand vista of the one life and unable to see the details.

If our "I am" is that of a separate individual, then we align with and are motivated by the purpose of an individual. Our identity and our purpose are exclusive. However, at this point the "I am" is nearsighted—focused on immediate details and unable to see the grand vista.

The result is illustrated by the following tale:

Once upon a time a mystic and an occultist were walking

the upward way on the Mount of Initiation. They walked the same path, for there was only the one, but their perspectives were so different that neither saw what the other saw.

The mystic sought liberation by losing his self in union with the divine. He kept his gaze fixed upward, toward the cloud shrouded heights, and constantly stumbled over roots and stones at his feet.

The occultist sought liberation via knowledge of the divine. He kept his gaze fixed on his surroundings, and constantly stopped to examine minute details of the path, such as the antics of a colony of ants.

The path is the same, but our experience of it is unique to us.

Since we relate purpose with matter and matter with purpose, we are responsible for the character and quality of the forms matter takes on. We create those forms, whether we are aware of it or not. In fact, our ignorance of the Law, up to now, has been something of a blessing.

Imagine a separative, self-centered humanity in which everyone knew how to consciously create the world they chose! The results would be catastrophic, far beyond anything we are capable of today. Thus, by limiting our destructive potential, our ignorance of the Law has saved us from our selves.

However, limited though we've been by our ignorance, we still wield the Law. We've still impressed our will on matter, and matter has responded.

As we've discussed, for the past several thousand years

humanity's spiritual paths have emphasized the path of ascension. These paths were typified by two primary characteristics:

1. The desire to escape the pain of life in the material world: After many ages of experience in realms of matter one slowly realizes that true happiness or joy cannot be known through wealth, power, sex, or any thing. One realizes that life in the world of form is one of pain, and one desires to escape that pain. One then begins seeking a way of escape. Sometimes the way discovered involves physical trials and deprivations, cultivating feelings such as bliss, or gathering knowledge and developing one's abstract intellect.

Flawed and incomplete though it is, this realization, and the resulting desire to escape, is a crucial stage in spiritual growth. It is at this point that one begins to turn one's attention beyond form to the greater life of which we are a part.

This stage can use virtually any form of matter as the stimulus. Any thought, feeling, or form, distorted by our separative identification with it, can propel us into this crisis. These can include drugs, belief systems, and a variety of inner practices. However, all of them share a basic flaw—one cannot escape the pain of individual life by denying that pain, but only by rejoining the greater life of which one is a part.

Thus, all attempts to escape one's own pain eventually fail, and one is forced to turn outside of one's separated self for release. This leads us to the second characteristic of our recent spiritual paths:

2. The aspiration to ascend to and unite with the one life: As one realizes the futility of escape, one turns outside of oneself to the greater life of which one is a part. During this stage, one traditionally aspired to and worked toward union or at-one-ment with the one life. The desire to escape became the aspiration to union.

The path of ascension was long and difficult, but it worked (for the individual). However, its benefits to the one life were relatively limited, and it created several problems.

Seekers on the path of ascension tend to view matter as an obstacle:

Those on the mystical path (liberation via right experience) tend to view the physical body and the intellect as obstacles to union. This often leads to practices designed to control the physical body and deny or suppress the intellect.

Those on the occult path (liberation via right knowledge) tend to view the physical body and the emotions as obstacles to union. This often leads to practices designed to control the physical body and suppress the emotions.

Thus, humanity identified matter—our bodies, emotions, and mind, as an obstacle to liberation. We identified matter as bad, and it believed us.

Our separated identity related our separated will to matter, and matter obeyed. Matter responded to our separation by creating forms that differentiated our bodies, emotions, and minds from the rest of the one life. Programmed to believe that it was bad, our matter opposed and resisted all attempts to reunite with the one life. In obedience to us:

> Matter responds to our separated will rather than the planetary purpose.

> Matter identifies as a separated individual rather than as a portion of the planetary life.

As we've seen, matter is not evil. It is as much a part of the one life as are purpose and consciousness. Matter is as divine as they, and the one life could not exist without it. Thus, all of our matter is divine, a part of the planetary life. Because of our individual identities we have differentiated our matter into apparently separate personalities, including physical, emotional, and mental natures. But, no matter how much it may deny and resist, our matter remains part of the one planetary life.

The separation and resistance of matter grew out of the normal, unconscious working of the Law of Relationship. Fortunately, it can be restored to its proper place and function by the right use of that Law. As we identify as individuals within the one life, we return our will, our consciousness, and our matter to that life.

As we return our will, consciousness, and matter, we realize that we have a purpose, place, and function within the one life. We realize that via the Law of Relationship we can help every one discover and take up their place within that life.

This is the new path of union or at-one-ment toward

which we are all working. It is a path that humanity is walking together, for the liberation of all. It includes the grand vista of the mystic and the minute details of the occultist. It synthesizes the three in all of us into a transformed one. Our will becomes part of divine will. Our consciousness becomes part of divine consciousness. Our matter becomes part of divine matter.

In the process, our separated matter is reprogrammed with its true place and function. Our matter then naturally cooperates with the planetary purpose, and our personas are transformed into vehicles of light.

Chapter 4

Awakening Humanity

These are the three aspects of the Law of Relationship—the motivating purpose of Spirit, the relationship of Consciousness, and the creative activity of Matter. When our purpose is part of the planetary purpose, when our identity is part of the planetary self, when our activity is a dedicated part of the planetary activity, then the effects will be in harmony with the planetary life.

When our motivating purpose, our identity, and our activity are within but separate from that life, then the results reflect that separation. This is the situation for most of humanity today, but it will not remain so for this is a time of Awakening!

Aligning our Spirit, Consciousness, and Matter with the Planetary Life

Sit comfortably, close your eyes, and relax your physical body.

Move your self awareness into your heart.

Calm your emotions by picturing them as a perfectly calm, clear pool of water in a forest glade.

Listen to the sounds of the forest. What do you hear?

Become aware of the variety of odors. What do you smell?

Gaze into the mirror-smooth pool and see there the reflection of the deep-blue sky.

Take a deep breath, and as you slowly release it recognize that your motivating purpose is part of the purpose of the planetary life.

Take another deep breath, and as you slowly release it recognize that your consciousness is part of the consciousness of the planetary life.

Take another deep breath, and as you slowly release it recognize that your every action is part of the activity of the planetary life.

Take another deep breath, and as you slowly release it recognize that your entire being is part of the planetary life.

Chapter 4

Align your purpose, consciousness, and activity with the planetary life by audibly sounding the OM.

Take a deep breath, and slowly open your eyes.

Chapter 4 Commentary

We are blessed to live at a time of realization, when we can transform separation into at-one-ment.

We will achieve that transformation by wielding the Law of Relationship. By practicing the Law in service to the planetary life we:

Align our personal will with divine will,

Align our individual identity with the planetary consciousness, and

Align our body, emotions, and mind with planetary matter.

This alignment process is quite simple and, with practice, easy to perform. However, in the beginning it may seem mysterious and difficult. This seeming will disappear as we gain experience with the process. In the meantime, we approach understanding through symbols and analogy. For instance, the alignment process can be compared to magnetizing a piece of iron.

Normally, the atoms in a piece of iron are not aligned— the poles of the iron atoms face in random directions. As a result, the magnetic fields of the atoms cancel each other out. However, if one repeatedly passes a magnet over or across a piece of iron, the poles of the atoms realign to face in the same direction. As a result, the magnetic fields of those atoms work together, and the iron itself becomes magnetic.

Chapter 4

As part of the one life, each individual iron atom embodies all three aspects of the one life. These are the three aspects of the Law of Relationship—the motivating purpose of Spirit, the relationship of Consciousness, and the creative activity of Matter. When our purpose is part of the planetary purpose, when our identity is part of the planetary self, when our activity is a dedicated part of the planetary activity, then the effects will be in harmony with the planetary life.

The basic characteristics of the three remain the same, whether they are the three of an atom, an individual, a nation, a species, or of the entire planetary life. The characteristics remain the same because it is the same three. They are the one, focused into the many yet remaining part of the planetary life.

That focus of the one into the many was necessary for the growth and development of the whole. In order to grow, the whole had to differentiate itself. We see this in the development of our own bodies, from a fertilized egg to a fully-formed infant.

The early fetal stem cells are undifferentiated. That is, they are capable of becoming part of any portion of the body. They may develop into brain, heart, skin, kidney, or nerve cells. However, they have not yet received and responded to a specific purpose, and thus have not yet differentiated themselves into a particular type of tissue.

As the stem cells receive and respond to that intent, they alter themselves into specific cell types. The ultimate result is a newborn babe, with a full set of cell types in a very complex body.

Had the stem cells remained undifferentiated, the complex body could not have come into being. Thus, differentiation is necessary to the development of a form that houses consciousness and expresses will.

The movement of the one into the many has often been portrayed as a fall from grace or from a divine state of union with the one life. While this is true, in a sense, it is only part of the truth. That movement of purpose and identity into matter was part of a process of growth that would not otherwise have been possible.

A single cell may be a one life, but its ability to think, feel, and act within the planetary life is very limited. However, if that same cell is fertilized with the full intent and consciousness of an individualized human soul, it can grow into a powerful vehicle for the one life.

Of course, before that vehicle can be effective, it must be aligned:

> The appetites and actions of the physical body must be aligned with each other and with the other portions of the personality. So long as they are not aligned, they will conflict with and work against each other, just like unaligned atoms—cancelling each other out and rendering us largely ineffective.

> The desires and aspirations of the emotions must be aligned with each other and with the rest of the personality. So long as our emotions are not aligned, they will conflict with and work against each other.

> The thoughts of the mind must be aligned with each other and with the emotions and physical body. So

long as our thoughts are not aligned, they will conflict with and work against each other.

So long as our thoughts, feelings, and physical bodies are not aligned, they will conflict with and work against each other.

In a sense, our lack of alignment has been a safety mechanism. It has limited our effectiveness, and thus our destructiveness, as unconscious creators within the planetary life. However, this protection is passing as humanity learns to become conscious creators. The question then becomes, what will we create?

Will we remain aligned with our own individualized purpose, and create separation and disharmony within the planetary life? Or will we align with the greater purpose, and help reunite the scattered portions of that life into a greater whole?

Will we help save Earth, or destroy it?

That is the question before us now, and in the following pages we will explore how we can save Earth together.

How to Serve Humanity

Chapter 5

Leaping Into At-one-ment

In order to wield the Law of Relationship to the benefit of the planetary life, rather than to its detriment, we must change. Up to now, this evolutionary leap (sometimes called enlightenment, cosmic consciousness, or at-one-ment) has been taken by individuals. However, our many problems, the products of our selfish creative activity, are forcing humanity to change *as one*.

We have created the opportunity for all of us to take that evolutionary leap together. If we do so, from then on every member of humanity will be aware of themselves as both an individual within the human kingdom, and as part of the one planetary life. Our purpose will be part of the planetary purpose, our consciousness will be part of the planetary consciousness, and our creative activity will be part of the planetary activity.

All of this is made not only possible, but necessary, by the many problems and difficulties we have created. We have placed our self in the position where the only way to solve our problems is by applying the Law of Relationship in service to the one planetary life. That practical application of the Law in service is the process by which we will take the leap into at-one-ment.

Leaping Into At-one-ment

Sit comfortably, close your eyes, and relax your physical body.

Move into your heart.

From your focus in the heart...

Calm your emotions.

Focus your attention on the spark of life within the heart. (pause)

Recognize that this spark of life is part of the fire of life of Earth.

Take a deep breath, and as you slowly release it expand your awareness to include the fire of life of the entire planetary life.

Take another deep breath, and leap into that fire.

Let your spark of life merge with that one life, and become that life.

Let your identity merge with the one life, and become one with it.

Take another deep breath, and as you slowly release it recognize that you are the planetary life.

As the One Life, *audibly sound (say)* the OM.

Take a deep breath, and slowly return to this time and place.

Chapter 5 Commentary

We are blessed to live when the long dark night is giving way to the light of our soul.

All human beings have the ability to change. That ability is derived from the one life of which we are a part.

Like everything else that exists, we are composed of the three aspects of divinity—divine purpose or will, divine love or wisdom, and divine matter or substance.

Uniquely within the planetary life, members of the human kingdom are self aware.

As we've seen, because of our self awareness we can use the Law of Relationship to transform the world. We have the unique ability to identify as the self or soul, and as the self to align purpose with substance and substance with purpose, bringing the two into at-one-ment. Substance responds by changing its motion, producing forms and activities that express that purpose. This is the method of conscious change.

All human beings are increasingly motivated to change. We are creating conditions in the world that are forcing us to realize that we must change our collective behavior. The rising tide of mass extinctions, epidemics, global warming, displaced populations, hunger, thirst—all of these are driving us to change.

That change begins with the expansion of our consciousness from that of the isolated individual to that of the larger life. The individual identity is not lost, it merely expands its scope or range. No matter how motivated we may be, this expansion must take place before we can change our behavior. So long as our consciousness is identified as an isolated individual—with individual thoughts, emotions, and behaviors—we will be unable to change those separative behaviors.

In order to transform our consciousness we must first detach from the old individual identity and patterns of thought, emotion, and behavior. We begin this detachment from the old by identifying as the consciousness or soul.

This can be compared to the way an inchworm moves from one leaf to another.

> The inchworm crawls along until it reaches the edge of the leaf it is on, lets go with its front feet while holding on with its back, stretches out across the intervening space to the next leaf, and grabs hold of the new leaf with its front feet. Then it lets go of the old leaf with its back feet, and pulls its backside up to the new leaf.

An inchworm typically moves from one leaf to another in quest for food. It has consumed all the edible portions of the previous leaf, all of it that it cares to eat, or it does not care for the taste of the leaf it was on.

We used to be able to move on as well, leaving used-up territory behind and taking over new. But now there are so many of us, and our behavior is so destructive, that we are quickly running out of consumables.

Chapter 5

More and more of us are realizing this. We are realizing that we cannot continue the old behaviors, that we must change our relationship with the world, and that the way to change our behavior and our relationship is to change our awareness of who we are.

This growing realization is powering an explosion of interest in methods of spiritual growth. More and more of us are seeking new and alternative methods of self-transformation. All of these methods offer something of use to their practitioners, otherwise we would lose interest and they would disappear. However, self transformation is not enough.

It is not enough, in this time of crisis and opportunity, to transform our selves one by one. It is not enough to stand up and declare, "I will awaken to the one life!" For the moment one does so, the moment one relates one's individual identity with the one life, one stimulates and strengthens that individual awareness as never before.

As a result one becomes, for a time, far more separative than one was. A classical example is the seeker who, determined to pursue the spiritual path, renounced all worldly ties—gave up their family, friends, associates, and possessions—dressed in rags, picked up a begging bowl, and left to seek a lonely life of contemplation in an isolated mountain cave.

Yes, one may escape the cares of the world and achieve great expansions of awareness very rapidly through such a course, but who does it serve? The awareness gained in isolated contemplation is not particularly useful to the rest of humanity. It has little practical application in the world of affairs and is of little use to the average householder.

One may argue that one will serve humanity when one has achieved enlightenment. But how would one more enlightened being help humanity help ourself?

Awakening one by one is too slow, and does little to solve the current crisis. How then shall we proceed? By walking the path together.

The problems we face today are common problems, and common opportunities. They bring us together in shared crisis, and help us:

Identify as humanity experiencing that crisis,

As humanity, align with the solution,

Align that solution with that condition,

Unite the solution and the condition in our collective consciousness,

Formulate that union into a practical plan of action, and

Carry out that plan of action together.

In the process, our consciousness becomes part of the planetary consciousness. Again, we retain our individual identities, but the range and scope of that identity expands far beyond its current limits.

Our individual motivations (goals, desires, and appetites) merge into one motivation, which becomes part of the purpose of the one life. Our motivating will becomes focused and empowered far beyond its current capacity.

Our personality (including mental, emotional, electrical, and physical vehicles) merge into an integrated whole, which becomes part of the substance of the one life. Our activities then become far more coherent and effective.

We become an integral part of the planetary life, taking our place and performing our function in service to humanity.

Having decided to serve, and having dedicated our self or soul to the one life, the next step is to immerse our self in the one and experience what we can of its unity.

The goal at this point is not to become one with the one, but to prepare our self for service by expanding our identity beyond its current limits. The more of the one we can identify with, the more of the one we can relate with. The more of the one we can relate with, the more of it we can serve through the Law of Relationship.

This, then, is our purpose in immersing our self in and awakening to the one life—in order to serve.

That purpose gives direction and meaning to our awakening process. We are doing this for the benefit of everyone within the one life. And as a result, the realization gained from our efforts is directly related to the current crisis. The awareness gained is extremely useful to humanity. It has immediate practical application in the world of affairs and is of great use to the average householder.

Thus, we are learning to use the Law of Relationship in service to the one life.

Chapter 6

The Illusion of Isolation

The first step in resolving a problem is to recognize that *we* have one. The next is to take responsibility for that problem. However, because of our individual motives and identity, we are unable to do either properly.

Our individual identity isolates us from the rest of the planetary life. This isolation was a necessary stage in the evolution of humanity. It enabled us to develop capacities (mental, emotional, etc.) that we need in order to perform our function in the planetary life, and which we would not otherwise have had. However, it is but a stage in our evolution, not the goal, and its consequences are forcing us to awaken to the greater life of which we are a part.

As isolated individuals, we automatically divide things into that which is "mine" (*my* idea, *my* feeling, *my* hunger), and that which is "not mine" (*their* idea, *their* feelings, *their* hunger). The same consciousness that identifies a book as "mine" or a house as "theirs" identifies a problem as "mine" or "theirs." As we shall see, this is an illusion, and the results are always harmful to the individuals involved and to the planetary life.

Awakening our Response-Ability

Sit comfortably, close your eyes, and relax your physical body.

Move into your heart.

From your focus in the heart...

Calm your emotions.

Take a deep breath, and as you slowly release it merge your motivating purpose with the purpose of the planetary life.

Recognize that you have the ability to respond to the planetary purpose.

Take another deep breath, and as you slowly release it merge your consciousness with the consciousness of the planetary life.

Recognize that you have the ability to be that planetary consciousness.

Take another deep breath, and as you slowly release it merge your activity with the activity of the planetary life.

Recognize that you have the ability to act as and within the planetary life, that you can create change.

Audibly sound the *OM*.

Take a deep breath, and slowly return to this time and place.

Chapter 6 Commentary

We are blessed to live at a time of responsibility, when we are recognizing that we can change the world.

Humanity has taken the first step in resolving our problems—recognizing that we have them.

More and more of us are becoming aware that the many problems that make up the world crisis—poverty, hunger, epidemics, pollution, climate change, etc.—are not local or regional, but global. These problems belong to all of us.

They belong to all of us not only because we all share them, but because we all contributed to them. The current world situation is not a cosmic accident. We created this crisis with our collective thoughts, desires, appetites, and actions.

So long as we identify as separate individuals, our thoughts, emotions, and behavior are out of harmony with the one life and harmful to it.

When we focus in the heart and align with the one life, then our thoughts, emotions, and behavior are in harmony with and support the one life.

Up to now, humanity has been identifying and behaving as separate individuals. And it is this common experience and shared responsibility that gives us hope of creating solutions.

How to Serve Humanity

Because we created this crisis, we can solve it.

If the current world crisis had been a cosmic accident, an event whose cause was beyond our control or influence, there might have been little we could do about it. However, since we are all directly responsible for the world condition, we all have the ability to transform it. Not individually, but collectively.

All we have to do is transform ourselves, and through our selves the world, using the Law of Relationship.

* * *

As we've discussed, this transformation begins with our identity and our awareness.

When we focus in the heart, we place ourselves in that part of our persona that is most receptive to the one life. From the heart, we can align with all of humanity, and identify as humanity within the one life.

Identified as humanity we can then relate with the purpose of the one life, or with any portion of that purpose.

As humanity, we can relate the purpose of the one life with any condition within that life.

As humanity, we can unite that condition with that purpose, transforming that condition.

Of course, one person or one small group cannot on its own solve the world's problems. The problems are simply too many and too pervasive for any group to solve. However, working together, a group can align with and manifest solutions to a problem, and make those solutions available to humanity.

Chapter 6

Take for instance the Law of Relationship itself. The fact of this Law was not realized by an individual, or by any one group, but by many members of humanity working over thousands of years.

The methods of using the Law were not developed by any one individual, but by many members of humanity also working for a very long time.

The Law has existed throughout humanity's history, has been given many names, and has been described in a variety of ways. Up to now, however, it has mostly been used by isolated individuals who renounced the world, withdrew into the lonely places, and practiced the Law in quest of at-one-ment with the one life.

In past ages this was right and proper. Most of humanity was caught up in their individual problems, and was in no condition to practice the Law. That is not the case today.

While we are still very much caught up in our problems, those problems are less and less viewed as ours alone, and more and more as those of humanity. Our daily lives are increasingly forcing us to recognize that we live in one vast life, that everything is related with everything else, and that in order to solve our problems we must all work together.

* * *

Of course, our individual experience with humanity tells us that we are completely unable to cooperate on anything. Fortunately, when practicing the Law of Relationship it is not necessary that we cooperate on anything. When practicing the Law, one is using a conscious, creative process to relate purpose with matter and matter with purpose. One is creating union or at-one-ment between these two aspects of divinity. That is all.

One is not attempting to prove the correctness of anyone's thoughts, validate anyone's feelings, or create any particular outer form.

When one is using the Law of Relationship in alignment with the one life:

Thinking is a result of the Law,

Feeling is a result of the Law,

Physical effects are a result of the Law.

They are a result, not a goal but a result.

Thus, when practicing the Law consciously, our attention is focused on the creative process. Not on any predetermined effects we'd like to produce, but on the process itself.

Any attempt to bring about a specific result—to get a job, help a political candidate win an election, win a lottery, find a mate, etc.—will only move one out of the higher identity, and out of the alignment between divine purpose and divine substance, dropping one back into the old, separative, individual identity.

Thus, in order to solve our problems, it is necessary to awaken from our individual self-awareness. In order to serve humanity, we must focus in the heart, relate divine purpose with divine substance, and at-one with the one life.

110

Chapter 7

Unlocking Your Creative Potential

We are all, each and every one of us, part of that one planetary life. We are all connected within that life, and what affects any one of us affects all of us. The appearance of isolated problems, individual or group, is an illusion created by the isolation of the separated self. As discussed later, it is not "my" problem or "your" problem. It is a condition within humanity that you have recognized because you have a relationship with it.

As lone individuals, we feel helpless before the larger life. This is a correct assessment. When we isolate ourselves from the one planetary life, we limit our creative potential. Our motivating power, ability to relate, and creative activity are restricted to those of our individual mind, emotions, and body.

Individuals react to these apparent limits in a number of ways. Many feel that they are powerless to change the world around them and thus are not responsible for the world's problems. However, this illusion merely disempowers them further as it robs them of the ability to respond creatively and effectively.

When we reject responsibility for a problem we renounce our *ability to respond*, to create change. How can we change, when we have surrendered our creative power to someone else?

Some react by aspiring to become powerful enough to

shape the world around them, according to their own motives, thoughts, and feelings. This is natural and necessary, for, as we shall see, a strong individual identity is required for the next step in evolution. We gain that power as we develop the clarity of our individual mind, the force of our individual feelings, and the abilities of our individual body. However, with greater power and effectiveness, come greater consequences. The negative effects of our creative efforts grow increasingly obvious.

Chapter 7

Dedicating our Body,
Emotions, and Mind
To the Planetary Life

Sit comfortably, close your eyes, and relax your physical body.

Move into your heart.

From your focus in the heart...

Calm your emotions.

Take a deep breath, and as you slowly release it dedicate your body to the planetary life.

Take another deep breath, and as you slowly release it dedicate your emotions to the planetary life.

Take another deep breath, and as you slowly release it dedicate your thoughts to the planetary life.

Take another deep breath, and as you slowly release it audibly state:

> *"I dedicate my entire persona—body, emotions and mind—to the one the planetary life."*

Audibly sound the *OM*.

Take a deep breath, and slowly return to this time and place.

Chapter 7 Commentary

We are blessed to live at a time of darkness, for it forces us to look for the light.

Imagine an infant of, say, 18 months. Its individual will and consciousness are very undeveloped, but focused on just a few things. Because it is so narrowly focused, the infant is much more causative to its environment than it would be otherwise. However, that causality is limited to its narrow area of interests.

Imagine a teenager of, say, 16 years. Their will, consciousness, and persona are much more developed than that of an infant (although it may not always appear so). But, their will is churned by powerful new appetites and desires, and their consciousness is confused by the attempt to form a mature identity. Their churning new appetites and desires are often so strong that they completely dominate their will and consciousness.

Teenage boys, for instance, typically "think about" sex almost constantly, and much of their behavior is driven by their desire and appetite for sex.

Imagine a young adult, with family, profession, and home, all demanding their attention. Their will, identity, and activities are divided among multiple responsibilities, each and all of which they feel must be met.

For instance, a young adult may make career decisions based on the needs of their family—choosing a career that enables them to pay for the home, education, and after-school activities their family needs, while leaving them the time to attend family activities such as soccer games.

At each level of growth, we develop more will, more self awareness, and more capacity to focus and direct our thoughts, emotions, and activities. As our will, consciousness, and persona develops, our identity becomes stronger as well.

As mentioned earlier, our "I"dentity is the result of the tendency of our consciousness to identify with some thing. When your consciousness in effect states, "I will to be ..." then your identity is that focus of will. If a teenager taking Driver's Ed. wills to be the best driver possible, then in that moment that focus of will is their identity. That identity focuses their will on being the best driver possible, and substance responds by working to give that will shape and form. This is the creative process in action.

If that teenager also thinks "I am a very bad driver," then at that moment that focus on a perceived condition is also part of their identity. Part of their "I will to be ..." is appropriated by that "I am ...", and used to motivate substance. Substance then responds by giving shape and form to their identity as a bad driver.

The usual result is a will, identity, and persona that is so confused by mixed motivations and activities, that it is very ineffective at accomplishing anything. In this condition, it does not really matter how much will, energy, force, or substance is available to the consciousness. That consciousness is so scattered that any attempted activity will be scattered and opposed by their own will, identities, and thoughts, desires and appetites.

The solution is to align the three—will, consciousness, and substance—giving them a common motivation, focus, and activity. The persona is then both more powerful in fact, and much more powerful in effect.

This realignment is accomplished via a simple application of the Law. One dedicates each aspect to the same motivating intent or purpose, thereby focusing all three aspects on that intent. One's portion of the will, consciousness, and substance of the one life then begin working together. If that motivating purpose is to serve the one life, then all the resulting effects will be in harmony with that life.

This strengthening is somewhat weakened when we surrender responsibility for our purpose or actions to someone or something else. This surrendering of responsibility occurs when we place ourselves in the type of subsidiary role where a separated person or group determines our purpose and directs our actions.

If a person or group sees themselves as separate from the one life, and we surrender our will to their will, then we weaken our individual will and cut ourselves off from the will of the one life. The collective will of such a group can be quite strong, even while the will of most of its members is comparatively weak. However, because of its separated focus the group purpose will be out of alignment with the planetary purpose and the effects of the group will be destructive to the one life.

This type of misalignment is seen in abundance today in

the many organizations whose purpose is to produce wealth for their stockholders. The resulting effects on the one life are a secondary consideration at best. The problem is not inherent in their organizational structure, but in their motivating purpose.

For instance, in the 19th century it was common to form "public benefit" corporations for a specific purpose (such as building a bridge), that would benefit the public and return a profit to the investors. If all corporations were organized for the public good, and had to continue to benefit the public in order to retain their charter, then the purpose of corporations could be aligned with the one life and they would benefit humanity as well as their investors.

In the absence of a worldwide rewrite of the corporate legal code, someone who is aligned with the one life, and part of an organization, can help realign that organization with the one life using the Law of Relationship. We will examine how to do this later in the course.

In the meantime, we are building the foundation for that type of group realignment work by realigning our own persona (body, emotions, and mind) with the one life. This automatically reduces or removes the influence of any separated groups we may belong to, releases our power and creative capacity, and prepares us to move within those groups as agents of the one life.

That is why, in this lesson, we dedicate our body, emotions, thoughts, and entire persona to the one life.

How to Serve Humanity

Section 2

The Law of Relationship

How to Serve Humanity

Chapter 8

Releasing Your Power

When we experience our self as part of the planetary life, that union expands our ability to move within and influence that life. The motivating power, ability to relate, and creative activity available to us is unlimited. We then recognize all problems as our problems, and take responsibility for them.

Fortunately, there is a way to transition from destructive individual motives to benevolent, inclusive motives. One begins by accepting that one is both an individual and part of a collective consciousness. Then, in aspiration to the one life of which one is a part, one wields the Law of Relationship in service to that life.

This is how we consciously take the next step in our spiritual growth and development—awaken to our purpose and place, and take up our function, within the one planetary life.

All of this is made possibly by the conscious, focused, and persistent use of the Law of Relationship.

Invoking our Purpose, Place and Function Within the Planetary Life

Sit comfortably, close your eyes, and move into your heart.

Take a deep breath, and as you inhale sense the one life flowing into your body.

Take another deep breath, and as you inhale sense the one life flowing into your emotions.

Take another deep breath, and as you inhale sense the one life flowing into your mind.

Take another deep breath, inhaling your purpose within the one life.

Take another deep breath, inhaling your place within the one life.

Take another deep breath, inhaling your function within the one life.

Audibly sound the *OM*.

Take a deep breath, and slowly return to this time and place.

Chapter 8 Commentary

We are blessed to live at a time when the nature and consequences of Divine Law are becoming clear.

The first step in taking up our purpose, place, and function in the one life is to be aware that we have them.

The second step is to align with our purpose, place, and function and call them into our lives.

Until we experience our purpose, place, and function, they remain abstract ideas. They remain thoughts that we may contemplate and discuss, but their relationship with our everyday lives remains theoretical.

We move from theory to reality by aligning with our purpose, place, and function, and calling them into appearance in our lives. That is the purpose of the current meditation. We are using the Law of Relationship to begin moving these three principles from abstract ideas to experienced realities.

This is only a beginning. The entire process will take more than one lesson, or any one course. However, you can obtain a basic foundation in the tools you will need—in the practice of the Law—by performing the meditations in *How to Serve Humanity* regularly and persistently.

As you perform the meditations, you will slowly learn to align with and become aware of your purpose, place, and function within the one life. This process works out differently for each of us. Some have a stronger sense of purpose, others are more aware of their place within or relationship to the one life, and others are more conscious of their function or activity within it. Sometimes this awareness unfolds gradually over time, and for others it comes in sudden bursts of enlightenment.

None of these are better than or to be desired above the others. Each is simply part of our individual way of awakening to our selves within the one life.

Purpose

As we awaken to our purpose, we become increasingly aware of our motives.

Individual: At first, we experience our motives as individual ideals, desires, and appetites.

Group: As we awaken, we slowly become aware that appetites, desires, and ideals are activities of the body, emotions, and mind, and that they are shared by all humanity. We become aware, for instance, that the desire for an ideal mate is not ours alone, but is shared by much of humanity. All desires are shared. They exist within humanity as a whole, with each member experiencing them to greater or lesser degrees depending on their particular tendencies.

As we become aware that the appetites, desires, and thoughts we experience are not ours, we free our selves from them. Their pull is greatly reduced, and they slowly cease to motivate us.

At about the same time (often simultaneously), we turn

our attention to motivations outside of our individual self. We become increasing aware of the purpose of the groups, communities, and nations of which we are a part. Slowly, their purpose becomes our purpose, their goals and motives become ours.

Humanity: Our motivating purpose gradually expands until it includes that of the human kingdom. At that point, our purpose is the growth and development of the consciousness of humanity—the awakening of every human being to the fact that they are soul.

Place

As we awaken to our place, we become increasingly aware of our self as the soul. At first, we experience our self as an individual that has a soul. Slowly, we become aware that we are a soul that has a personality.

As our awareness as soul expands, we become increasingly aware of our relationship as soul with and within the planetary life. We slowly realize that we have a particular relationship with the one life, and that this relationship is shared by other souls who have the same purpose and function within it.

We then realize that those souls who have the same purpose, relationship, and function are actually a group soul, a single being composed of many souls—a single being that is a portion of the soul of humanity, with a purpose, place, and function within the one life. Thus, our soul is the soul of humanity, differentiated from the whole by its relationship with a portion of the planetary purpose and activity.

Function

At first, our activities are directed by our individual identity and its motivating desires and appetites. However, as we awaken our activities gradually expand in scope. We continue to meet our immediate personal needs (for food, shelter, companionship, recreation, etc.), but the motivating purpose behind those activities changes. In addition, we begin new activities that directly express our purpose and place.

Like purpose and place, our activities tend to unfold in an expansion from the immediate individual, through family, group, community and nation, to the entire human kingdom. As our awareness grows, the motivating purpose and focusing consciousness behind all these activities becomes increasingly inclusive.

Purpose, Place, and Function

Individual Purpose, Place, and Function: So long as we are identified as individuals, the power of our motivating purpose, the focus of our consciousness, and the scope of our activities appear extremely limited. When we focus our will on an activity, it is our individual will, focused by our individual consciousness, on our personal activity. In essence, we become the neck of the hourglass through which everything must flow, greatly restricting both the amount and rate of activity, and thus how much can be accomplished.

Group Purpose, Place, and Function: As our awareness expands into group consciousness, the power of our motivating purpose, the focus of our consciousness, and the scope of our activities expands to that of the entire group. When we focus our will on an activity, it is our group will, focused by our group consciousness, on a group function within the human kingdom. In effect, the neck of the hourglass is expanded, greatly increasing both the amount and rate of flow, and thus how much can be accomplished.

Kingdom Purpose, Place, and Function: As our awareness expands into the consciousness of the entire human kingdom, the power of our motivating purpose, the focus of our consciousness, and the scope of our activities expands to that of the kingdom as well. When we focus will on an activity, it is the will of humanity, focused by a portion of the human consciousness on a function of the human kingdom within the one life. Figuratively speaking, the neck of the hourglass is eliminated, and so are the limits on the amount and rate of flow, and on how much can be accomplished.

This is how we release our power, by awakening our awareness of our purpose, place, and function within the one life. As we proceed, we will continue to expand our awareness, and release our power, by practicing the Law of Relationship.

How to Serve Humanity

Chapter 9

The Power to Create

The following pages offer the opportunity to perform and study the Law of Relationship. When you take up the Law, and what you do with it, is entirely up to you. However, having read these pages, you will no longer be able to proceed in ignorance. You will no longer be able to claim that you are powerless, that you are not able to respond to the problems that surround you. You will have the power to create whatsoever you will.

The Law of Relationship gives us the power to create because *it is power*. It is the motivating power of Spirit, the relationship of consciousness, and the creative activity of Matter. Utilizing these three—"Spirit," "Consciousness," and "Matter"—it is possible to define the Law as follows:

> *Everything that exists, in order to exist, must be three things—a motivating purpose, a relating consciousness, and an expressing activity.*[4]

The source of motivating purpose is sometimes called *"Spirit."* The planetary spirit is the source of the purpose, power, and will of the entire planetary life. The planetary purpose includes the purpose of every kingdom

---

[4] The Law of Relationship is virtually identical to the scientific "Law of Electromagnetism." The basic elements are the same, but where the Law of Electromagnetism describes the characteristics of electromagnets, the Law of Relationship describes the basic characteristics of everything that exists.

in nature (mineral, plant, animal, and human) and of every individualized soul within that life.

Likewise, the planetary power and will includes the power and will of every kingdom in nature, and of every individualized soul within the planetary life. Thus, our individual will is part of the will of the planetary life. As we awaken, we become aware that our purpose, power, and will is part of, rather than separate from, that of the one life. Our purpose, power, and will is seen and experienced as a portion of the planetary will—a portion with which we are related and for which we are responsible.

We will discuss the purpose, power, and will of Spirit in more detail as we proceed. However, our focus will be on aligning our individual purpose with planetary purpose, our power with planetary power, our will with planetary will, and acting in the world from that alignment.

Chapter 9

Aligning our Purpose, Place and Function With the Planetary Life

Sit comfortably, close your eyes, and move into your heart.

Take a deep breath, and relax your body.

Take another deep breath, and calm your emotions.

Take another deep breath, and focus your mind.

Take another deep breath, and as you exhale feel your motivating purpose moving out into the purpose of the one life.

Take another deep breath, and as you exhale feel your sense of place moving out into the one life.

Take another deep breath, and as you exhale feel your every activity moving out into the activity of the one planetary life.

Audibly sound the OM.

Take a deep breath, and slowly return to this time and place.

Chapter 9 Commentary

We are blessed to live at a time when each and all of us must find our purpose in the one planetary life.

The concept that everything is one is an abstract idea—until we experience the one in our heart.

The concept that the one is three is an abstract idea—until we experience the three in our heart.

Part of the problem we have with the concept of the one-that-is-three is that our rational mind is accustomed to thinking sequentially. Thus, the intellect expects one of the three to come first, and to generate the others. Actually, however, the one comes into being as a one, with each of the three already born full-grown within it.

In ancient times the one-that-is-three was portrayed, as always in the ancient mysteries, via symbol and allegory. Typically, the three were portrayed as a symbolical family.

Spirit was portrayed as a Divine Father.

Consciousness or Soul was portrayed as a Divine Child (as a daughter and as a son)

Matter was portrayed as a Divine Mother.

The use of the three, when wielding the Law of Relationship, was portrayed in ancient myths.

The Divine Father pronounced His Purpose and Will.

Chapter 9

The Divine Son conveyed the Will of the Father to the Divine Mother.

The Divine Mother responded with creative activity.

The Divine Daughter conveyed the fruits of that activity to the Father.

The patriarchism of recent ages shifted the emphasis of these myths to the male characters, throwing the myths out of balance. However, this is being corrected as we move into a proper understanding of the one life and its three aspects.

In modern times we have other symbols, such as that of the electro magnet. Basically, the Laws of Electromagnetism state that:

> If you have one pole you must have two poles. Thus, in order for a positive magnetic pole to exist, the negative pole must exist also (and vice versa).

> The two poles must be equal in strength. The positive pole must be equal in strength to the negative, and the negative equal to the positive.

> There must be a magnetic field between the two poles.

> The strength of the magnetic field is determined by the strength of the two poles and their distance from each other.

While the Laws of Electromagnetism were only meant to describe the workings of electromagnets, they are equally applicable to the three aspects of the one life.

If you have one pole you must have two poles. Thus, in order for Spirit or Matter to exist, the other must exist also.

The two poles must be equal in strength: Spirit (the Divine Father) must be equal in strength to Matter, and Matter (the Divine Mother) must be equal in strength to the Father.

There must be a field of relationship (consciousness or soul) between the two poles.

The strength of the field of relationship (the degree of consciousness or awareness) is determined by the strength of the two poles and their nearness to each other.

Through this last point, we see a clear hint of how the Law of Relationship works. As the field of relationship, the consciousness strengthens the two poles by bringing them into closer relationship to each other.

The consciousness relates spirit with matter, bringing the activity of matter into closer alignment with its motivating purpose.

The consciousness relates matter with spirit, bringing the motivating will of spirit into closer alignment with its creative activity.

As this process proceeds, spirit and matter are gradually brought into closer and closer relationship, intensifying their consciousness. At some point (long before the three become one) the seeker awakens to their true purpose, place, and function within the one life.

Chapter 10

Creative Activity

The source of creative activity is sometimes called *"Matter."* The planetary matter is the source of energy, force, and activity of the entire planetary life. It is the stuff of which everything is made, including the mental thoughts, emotional feelings, and electric patterns of every kingdom in nature and of every individualized soul within that life.

Thus, our individual matter (including our energy, force, and forms) is part of the matter of the planetary life. As we awaken, we become aware that our thoughts, feelings, and actions are part of, rather than separate from, that of the one life. Our thoughts, feelings, and actions are seen and experienced as a portion of the planetary matter—a portion with which we are related and for which we are responsible.

We will discuss the energy, force, and activity of Matter in more detail as we proceed. However, our focus will be on aligning our energy, force, and activity with planetary will.

Aligning our Energy, Force and Activity With Planetary Will

Sit comfortably, close your eyes, and move into your heart.

Take a deep breath, and relax your body.

Take another deep breath, and calm your emotions.

Take another deep breath, and focus your mind.

Take another deep breath, and as you inhale feel and see your mind filling with the energy of planetary purpose.

Take another deep breath, and as you inhale feel and see your emotions filling with the force of planetary purpose.

Take another deep breath, and as you inhale feel and see your body being activated by planetary purpose.

Recognizing that your body, emotions, and mind are aligned with the purpose of the planetary life, *audibly sound (say)* the *OM*.

Take a deep breath, and as you release it slowly return to this time and place.

Chapter 10 Commentary

We are blessed to live at a time when we are being forced to realize our potential.

Remember the magnet analogy, and the principal that everything that exists, in order to exist, must be three things—a positive pole, a negative pole, and a magnetic field between them? We initially used that universal law to understand the nature and relationship of spirit, consciousness, and matter. However, it is equally applicable to each of these three.

Matter, for instance, consists of the trinity of energy, force, and substance. This trinity of matter may be illustrated by the following story:

> Many years ago, a family visited the Craters of the Moon National Monument, in Idaho State. While there, they stopped for lunch at a scenic picnic spot. After they ate, the boys went exploring and discovered a trail up the side of a vertical cliff. They scrambled up, and when they finally reached the top the boys gazed down, and around at the top of the cliff. There, perched in a dish-shaped depression on the very edge, they discovered a huge, egg-shaped balancing boulder—about the size of a semi truck.
>
> Wondering if he could move it, one of the boys pushed against the boulder as hard as he could, and it rocked ponderously away from him, and back. The other boys joined in, pushing in time with the motion

of the boulder, slowly increasing the rocking motion, until the rocking edge of the boulder reached the lip of the depression in which it sat.

Then the boulder stopped increasing its motion. The lip of the depression was too steep, and they could force it no further.

Secretly relieved that their adventure had caused no harm, the boys returned to the picnic area.

Energy is potential. Because of its position at the top of the cliff, the boulder was a supply of kinetic energy, or potential activity. Other types of potential include ideas or thoughts.

Force is activity. If the boulder had been pushed over the cliff, its potential would immediately have been transformed into activity as the boulder rushed toward the bottom of the cliff. Activity is the relationship between potential and effect. Other types of activity include emotional feelings (not the resulting behavior, but the activity that produces it).

Physical matter is the effect or appearance. If the boulder had crashed to the ground, it would have crushed anything it landed on, and left a large dent. That would have been the effect in matter. We are all, of course, familiar with a wide variety of types of matter, including solids, liquids, gases, etc. From this perspective, all of those, any thing we can perceive with our senses, are effects or matter.

Of course, while the story portrays the trinity of potential, activity, and appearance as unfolding sequentially, they actual exist together.

Chapter 10

The magnetic poles of potential and appearance are always in balance, kept in right relationship by the magnetic field of activity. This must be so, for the Law of Relationship is at work here just as it is in the relationship between spirit, consciousness, and matter.

Our conscious use of the Law enables us to recreate that balance. We simply relate a specific potential to a specific appearance (thereby moving that potential into that appearance), by applying the proper force. When the force (or push) is applied at the right time and place, and in the proper rhythm, it is possible to produce very large transformations.

How to Serve Humanity

Chapter 11

The Soul of Creativity

The second aspect of the Law is sometimes called *"Consciousness"* or *"Soul."* The planetary consciousness is the magnetic field of relationship between the Spirit and Matter of the one life. It is the identity or self awareness of everything in that life, including the soul of every kingdom in nature and of every individualized soul within that life.

Thus, our individual self is part of the one soul of the planetary life. As we awaken, we become aware that our individual consciousness is part of, rather than separate from, that of the one consciousness. Our individual identity is not lost, but experienced as a portion of the planetary consciousness—a portion with a purpose, place, and function within that life.

We will discuss consciousness in more detail as we proceed. However, our focus will be on identifying as soul within the one life, and relating purpose with matter and matter with purpose, so that the two poles become one. This is the Law in action, the creative process through which we serve humanity.

Identifying as Soul Within
the Planetary Life

Sit comfortably, close your eyes, and move into your heart.

Slowly take a breath, and relax your body.

Slowly take another breath, and calm your emotions.

Slowly take another breath, and focus your mind.

Take another deep breath, and as you inhale feel the light and love of the planetary soul flowing into your heart.

Take another deep breath, and as you release it feel your own soul radiating light and love into the planetary life.

Take another deep breath, and feel the light and love of the soul flowing into and out from your heart.

Recognize that you are a self-aware soul within the one planetary soul.

Audibly sound the OM.

Take a deep breath, and slowly return to this time and place.

Namaste.

142

Chapter 11 Commentary

We are blessed to live at a time when each and all of us must find our self in the one planetary life.

We have already discussed the nature of consciousness or soul at some length, describing it as the magnetic field of relationship between spirit and matter. However, not only is soul the relationship between spirit and matter, it is also the source of the ability to relate.

Spirit, matter, and consciousness each have distinctive characteristics or qualities:

Spirit provides purpose, motivation, and direction.

Matter provides potential, activity, and appearance.

Consciousness provides relationship, awareness, and understanding.

Since it is born from the relationship between spirit and matter, and in fact is that relationship, a primary characteristic of the soul is the ability to relate. The soul can relate with any purpose, motivation, or direction of spirit, or with any potential, activity, or appearance of matter.

Since the soul is self awareness, a primary characteristic of the soul is the ability to be aware of anything and everything with which it is related. Thus, it is from the consciousness or soul that we gain the ability to be aware of our relationships—with family, friends, associates, organizations, ideas, emotions, etc.

Since the soul is the awareness of how things are related, a primary characteristic of the soul is the ability to understand. We truly understand something when, and only when, we perceive its relationship to the purpose and activity of the one life. Thus, the ability to perceive how something is related to the one life is the capacity to understand.

These abilities of the soul are moderated by our focus of identity. When we identify as a separated individual, our ability to relate, to be aware, and to understand are limited to those of that individual.

When we identify as a group, our ability to relate, to be aware, and to understand are expanded to those of that group.

When we identify as a kingdom, our ability to relate, to be aware, and to understand are expanded to those of that kingdom.

Another characteristic of the soul is the ability to identify. Earlier we defined the soul or consciousness as self awareness. Self awareness is the act of identifying the self as who and what one is. This awareness of self may begin as a simple awareness that one is a consciousness that has a body, emotions, and mind, it may come as a sudden burst of realization, or it may come through some combination of slow realization and sudden bursts. In any case, this capacity of the soul to identify as the self is not limited to self awareness.

The soul can identify with or as anything. It identifies *with* something when it is aware of relationship and identifies that relationship as being part of who and what it is. This produces a sense of attachment and possession, as in "my family," "my car," "my house," etc.

The soul identifies *as* something when it focuses on that thing as being part of who and what it is. Identifying as the thing itself is more intimate than identifying as the relationship with that thing, and usually produces a much more powerful sense of attachment. We can discover the things we are identified as by observing our response to the question, "Who are you?"

When asked, "Who are you?" questions, most of us respond with our name, gender, age, etc. All of these responses are the result of our identifying with those things. When we think, "I am," what comes up is our name, gender, age, height, hair color, all of those things that we identify as. We are, of course, none of these. They are things that are passing through our life, not who or what we are.

Who we are is soul, a part of the soul of the one life with a purpose, place, and function within that life. We begin the process of serving that function by identifying as soul, by thinking "I am soul." Then, as soul in the one life, we relate a condition in the world with its purpose, and its purpose with that condition, and bring the two into at-one-ment. We serve by practicing the Law of Relationship.

How to Serve Humanity

Chapter 12

Serving the Planetary Life

Each and all of us practice the Law of Relationship, and are responsible for the results. When we are ignorant of the Law, and wield it unconsciously, we cannot see the relationship between our individual purpose and its effects in our life and affairs. But, we are still responsible for our role in creating that life. When we are aware of the Law, and wield it consciously, the relationship between our will and our life is obvious.

When you wield the Law or Relationship consciously, you can no longer deny responsibility. You are aware of what you are doing when you wield it, and can see the results in your life and affairs. You then feel responsible—both empowered and accountable.

If you continue to act from selfish motives, that accountability becomes a heavy weight. A normal reaction is to attempt to justify our motives by creating "reasons" for why we think, feel, and act selfishly. However, the consequences of our behavior eventually reveal the delusion of those justifications.

If you fail to act, to help the world when you know you can, that responsibility festers. A normal reaction is to create "reasons" why we cannot act *now*. We tell ourselves that we would serve "if only"—if only we had the time, if only the children were grown, if only we knew what to do... However, the consequences of failing to act eventually reveal this disempowering delusion.

When you act as part and for the benefit of the greater life, that responsibility empowers you. A normal initial response is to create an outer service activity—something our personality finds interesting, attractive, and satisfying. We tell ourselves that whatever we are ready to do, that we enjoy doing, or that no one else is doing, must be *our* service activity. However, if the inner creative process is not performed first (relating a problem with the overshadowing planetary purpose, and that purpose with the embodied condition), then the service activity will not be in harmony with the planetary life.

Thus, the first step in finding our purpose and taking up our function within the planetary life is to perform the creative process.

Chapter 12

Performing the Creative Process –
Aligning Planetary Purpose
with our Life and Affairs
And Our Life and Affairs
with Planetary Purpose

Sit comfortably, close your eyes, and move into your heart.

Slowly take a breath, and relax your body.

Slowly take another breath, and calm your emotions.

Slowly take another breath, and focus your mind.

Take another deep breath, and as you <u>inhale</u> feel and see your life filling with the energy of planetary purpose.

Slowly inhale, and in the <u>pause</u> between breaths feel the planetary purpose in your heart.

Take another deep breath, and as you <u>exhale</u> feel and see the purpose in your heart radiating outward into the planetary life.

Slowly exhale, and in the <u>pause</u> between breaths feel the purpose within the entire planetary life.

Recognizing that your motivating purpose is aligned with the planetary life, and the planetary purpose is aligned with you...

Audibly sound the OM.

How to Serve Humanity

Take a deep breath, and as you release it slowly return to this time and place.

Namaste.

Chapter 12 Commentary

We are blessed to live at a time when we can serve humanity wherever we are and whatever we are doing.

Performing the inner creative process *is* the service activity. As a result, where you are and what you are doing in the outer world does not affect your ability to serve. You can serve anywhere while doing anything, so long as you practice the Law of Relationship while doing so.

When we perform the Law throughout our daily life, we transform our entire life and affairs into a ceremony, a ceremony of service to the one life. At that point, everything we do, no matter how "ordinary" in the outer sense, is a service activity.

We may, somewhat arbitrarily, divide our activities into ordinary daily activities and service activities.

Ordinary daily activities would include sleeping, bathing, eating, washing dishes, cleaning our home, driving to work, and all the other things most of us do in our daily lives. There is a tendency to dismiss these as potential service activities. Yet, they are a vital part of our life, and as we transform their character and quality we help transform the daily life of humanity. This is necessary, for it is as humanity holds the realization of the soul in the heart, during our daily life, that we will transform the one life.

As we develop the capacity to do so, it becomes our

response-ability to model this realization for humanity. Thus, one can serve humanity by holding a focus in the heart, aligning upward with the one life, and outward with humanity, while washing the dishes.

So long as we perform an activity, any activity, while aligned with its purpose within the one life, and with that portion of humanity who perform that activity (bringing purpose and activity into at-one-ment), then whatever we are doing is a service activity.

There are also those inner and outer activities that we perform specifically in order to be of service. Often it is in response to some unusual event, such as a disaster, war, accident, illness, or argument. At those times we may perform a single quick alignment, or a series of alignments for a set period or until the crisis is resolved. Occasionally we are attracted to specific conditions within humanity that will require months, years, decades, or lifetimes of work.

Because we tend to approach these activities, from the beginning, with the motivating intent to serve, there is a greater tendency to think of them as "service activities." These activities may be in the areas of leadership, education, healing, organization, commerce, art, media, religion, spirituality, etc.

The more time and reordering of our life we give to these activities, the more we tend to identify with them. Thus, we come to think of ourselves as leaders, teachers, healers, business persons, financiers, artists, ministers, spiritual seekers, etc.

While it is true that each soul has its purpose and

function within the one life, that function is an activity of the consciousness and not of the form. Because of its purpose and function, a soul will have a greater affinity for and work with a particular character and quality of the one life. These divine characteristics and qualities are described in different ways in different systems, and we will explore them to some extent in the second half of this course. The point to keep in mind now is that the inner activity of the soul is subjective. While it may be reflected for a time in a particular outer activity or profession, that activity is only a reflection of the reality.

Thus, we have what are somewhat arbitrarily identified as two types of service activities: via our daily life, and via ordered service activities.

To the extent that one is identified as separate from the whole, one will tend to be dissatisfied with service through one's daily life.

To the extent that one is identified as the whole, one will tend to reject ordered service activities as unnecessary.

However, complete service to the one life comes from discovering one's purpose, place, and function as an individual, as a group, and as a kingdom within the one life.

How to Serve Humanity

Chapter 13

Awakening to the Planetary Life

The first step in the creative process is also a step in awakening to one's true self—the consciousness or soul. Having long been identified with our individual thoughts, feelings, and sensations, we slowly realize that our thoughts, feelings, and sensations are not ours alone, but part of those of a greater life of which we are a part.

This awareness may dawn slowly, burst forth in a mystical realization, or arise through mental exercise. Those reading these pages are almost certainly aware of the planetary life to some extent, and are likely seeking their place and function within that life. That place and function is your birthright—part of who and what you are.

Invoking our Purpose, Place and Function Within the Planetary Life

Sit comfortably, close your eyes, and move into your heart.

Slowly take a breath, and relax your body.

Slowly take another breath, and calm your emotions.

Slowly take another breath, and focus your mind.

Take another deep breath, and as you <u>inhale</u> feel and see the energy of planetary purpose flowing into you, filling your heart with your purpose within the planetary life.

Slowly inhale, and in the <u>pause</u> between breaths sense, in your heart, your place within the planetary life.

Take another deep breath, and as you <u>exhale</u> feel and see your function radiating out, from your heart, into the planetary life.

Slowly exhale, and in the <u>pause</u> between breaths dedicate yourself to [living] your purpose, place, and function within the planetary life.

Audibly sound the OM.

Take a deep breath, and slowly return to this time and place.

Namaste.

Chapter 13 Commentary

We are blessed to live at a time when we are being forced to pay attention to what we are breathing.

You will have noted that we have begun using the cycles of our breath in our inner work. There are a number of possible purposes for becoming conscious of breathing, including:

Becoming more aware: When we focus on any portion of the form, particularly on its rhythms, we tend to become more aware of them. This increased awareness of a thing makes it possible to change it. In the case of breath this includes breathing more deeply and efficiently (diaphragmatic breathing), alternate-nostril breathing (to balance the subtle energy of the breath), etc. There is a danger, however, in such practice, as increased focus on the form can easily become increased identification with that form. Fortunately, this danger is easily avoided by maintaining one's intent on becoming conscious of and as the soul.

Mindfulness through breathing: It is also possible to use the breath as a focus for contemplation. This is often done using a candle, but the breath can work as well. In this technique one focuses one's entire attention on the breath or candle flame, becoming aware of it and nothing else. One then holds that focus of awareness for as long as possible, renewing it whenever the attention wavers. This process develops the ability to hold a focus of awareness. That ability is sometimes called "mindfulness" and is an essential part of the practice of the Law of Relationship. The ability to focus is transferable, that is, once we develop the ability to focus on one thing, we have the ability to focus on any thing, including on the relationship of a thing with its purpose. Thus, through contemplation we develop one of the abilities we need to perform the Law.

Cycles of the Creative Process: The creative process follows a rhythm that mirrors the rhythm of the breath. Like the breath, there is a movement inward, a pause, a movement outward, and a second pause. As a result, it is sometimes possible to use the rhythm of the breath (and other rhythms in nature) to augment the creative process. With the breath, one not only gains the assistance of a natural cycle, but also the sensations of that cycle. When included in the creative process, those sensations (of inward and outward movement) add to the reality of the experience, making it more effective. This is why we have begun including the breath in our inner work. At this point, from our focus in the heart, with an alignment up through the head and out from the heart, we:

Inhale the energy of planetary purpose into our heart

Pause to sense our place in the one life

Exhale our function into the one life

Pause and dedicate our self to our purpose, place, and function within the one life.

This process can be performed in a single cycle of the breath, but it will probably be easier to perform it over a number of cycles. For instance, while relaxed, calm, and

Chapter 13

breathing slowly, one may:

Focus on the inhale of seven breaths, then

Focus on the pause after the inhale of seven more breaths, then

Focus on the exhale of seven breaths, then

Focus on the pause after the exhale of seven breaths.

As one does this, each point in the cycle adds to the next. Each inhale adds to the next inhale, each pause adds to the next pause, each exhale adds to the next exhale, and each cycle of in-out adds to the next. This process, called resonance, is demonstrated in the childhood game of creating waves in a swimming pool.

While standing in the shallow end of a backyard swimming pool, holding a rigid-foam belly board, a child leaps up and pushes down on the board as they descend. Waves move out from the board, bounce off the side of the pool, and head back toward the child. The child leaps again, pushing down on a wave just as it passes beneath their board, adding more energy to that wave. Again and again the child leaps, adding more and more energy to the waves, until the waves grow so large that they flow over the top of the pool and onto the deck.

Our performance of the Law of Relationship is made much more effective when we use resonance—repeating the cycle of the creative process over and over, adding the energy and force from the earlier cycles to the later ones. When we do this together, it becomes possible for relatively small groups to help bring about large transformations.

How to Serve Humanity

We will discuss resonance further as we proceed, for it is a very important part of how we will serve humanity.

Chapter 14

Awakening One's Place and Function Within the Planetary Life

On a typical day we may place our inner point of attention in any of a number of locations (such as our tummy, diaphragm, heart, throat, and head), experiencing a different type of awareness in each. We will observe these various states of consciousness, including the purpose and function of each state, as we learn to perform the creative process.

Remember our definition of the Law of Relationship?

Everything that exists, in order to exist, must be three things—a motivating purpose, a relating consciousness, and an expressing activity.

Thus, every state of awareness or quality of consciousness must also have motivating will and expressing matter.

Every quality of consciousness is overshadowed by its portion of the planetary spirit. That spirit is the source of the purpose, power, and will of that consciousness, and (like a magnetic field, moving energy from one magnetic pole to another) the consciousness relates that purpose to matter.

Thus, consciousness relates spirit to itself.

161

Relating Spirit with Consciousness

Sit comfortably, close your eyes, and move into your heart.

Slowly take a breath, and relax your body.

Slowly take another breath, and calm your emotions.

Slowly take another breath, and focus your mind.

Take another deep breath, and as you inhale feel and see the purpose, power, and will of spirit flowing into your heart.

Sense that purpose filling your consciousness.

Sense that power filling your soul.

Sense your self becoming a center of planetary will.

Audibly sound the OM.

Take a deep breath, and slowly return to this time and place.

Namaste.

Chapter 14 Commentary

We are blessed to live at a time when each and all of us must find our purpose in the one planetary life.

During an ordinary day, we may find our self in a variety of places and states of awareness within our body. Some of these locations, such as the top of the head, forehead, throat, heart, and solar plexus are associated with specific states of awareness and types of energy. In fact, the state of awareness associated with the heart is why we place our self there during our inner work.

While the state of at-one-ment we utilize in the heart could be experienced from any point within the body, its long association with the heart makes at-one-ment most easily accessible from that position.

We could spend a great deal of time discussing the various points in the body—how they are formed, how they function, their structure, their different states of consciousness, how they are used, etc.—but that information is available in other works and is of little use in our present work.

Perhaps the simplest and most useful explanation of the heart is that it is a point of balance within the human energy system. It is the midway point between the overshadowing divine purpose and soul (contacted through the top of the head) and the outer material world.

As the midway point, the heart is the intermediary between

163

the two. From there, one has equal access both up to the divine and out to the material, up to the one life and out to the individual.

That is why we begin our work from a focus in the heart. From there we have access to a broader portion of the human spectrum of consciousness and energy than from anywhere else.

Chapter 15

Aligning the Planetary Purpose

Every quality of consciousness relates its portion of planetary spirit to matter. The matter is motivated by the purpose, power, and will of spirit into new activity. This is how new thoughts, feelings, and ways of being are born in the world, but it is also when the consciousness may identify with the form, lose its self, and become trapped in its creation.

Thus, *consciousness relates spirit to matter.*

Relating Spirit with Matter

Sit comfortably, close your eyes, and move into your heart.

Slowly take a complete breath, and relax your body.

Slowly take another complete breath, and calm your emotions.

Slowly take another complete breath, and focus your mind.

Take another deep breath, and as you inhale feel and see the purpose, power, and will of spirit flowing into your heart.

Sense that purpose filling your mind.

Sense that power filling your emotions.

Sense your personality becoming a center of planetary will.

Audibly sound the OM.

Take a deep breath, and as you release it slowly return to this time and place.

Namaste.

Chapter 15 Commentary

We are blessed to live at a time when we must differentiate between who we are and what we have.

So long as we practice the Law of Relationship unconsciously, the forms we create are obstacles to the purpose and plan of the one life. As mentioned before, all human beings are natural practitioners of the Law. We naturally align with purpose, and relate that purpose with substance. Substance then automatically responds by taking on a new movement, thereby creating a new form. This is how new forms are created.

When we create unconsciously, our creative activity is unconscious because we have identified our self as being separate from the one life. We believe we have our own purpose, consciousness, and forms, separate and apart from those of the planetary life. Since we are not aware of our relationships with the one life, we often create automatically, without reference to purpose, awareness, or substance beyond those of our immediate persona. This inevitably produces forms and activities that are out of harmony with and damage the one life.

As we begin to become aware of our self as a soul within the one life, we begin to see how damaging the forms around us are to that life. This dawning awareness produces a tendency to reject all form as oppositional to our higher purpose as a part of that life.

We may begin to see the world of affairs, and all it

contains, as obstacles to the spiritual path.

We may begin to see the emotional realm, and all the forces it contains, as obstacles to the path.

We may begin to see the mental realm, and all the energies it contains, as obstacles to the path.

A common reaction is to attempt to withdraw from any and all relationships with those realms and forms that one identifies as obstacles. However, the moment one identifies any of these energies, forces, or forms as inherent obstacles, then one makes oneself unable to use the energies so identified as anything but obstacles.

If one says, "all rational thought is an obstacle to realization," then the substantial energy of thought will believe you. You may not be aware of it, but you are using the Law when you make such a statement, and if you impress the energy of thought with the purpose or intent to be an obstacle then it will do its best to be an obstacle. The same is true of emotional force and outer forms.

Humanity has been creating obstacles for itself in this way for a very long time. Fortunately, this process is not without some benefit. It teaches us how to impress energy, force, and form with an intent, and it teaches us how to overcome obstacles. Once we have learned the lessons of creativity and perseverance, we are ready to begin identifying as the self or soul of humanity, to invoke the purpose of the one life, and to transform the obstacles into vehicles of the planetary purpose.

This is the function of the Law of Relationship when practiced consciously in service to the divine plan.

Chapter 16

Aligning Planetary Spirit and Matter

Every quality of consciousness relates its portion of planetary matter to itself. This slowly transforms the mind, emotions, and body from a prison into an instrument of the consciousness.

Thus, *consciousness relates matter to itself.*

Relating our Persona with our Self

Sit comfortably, close your eyes, and move into your heart.

Slowly take a complete breath, and relax your body.

Slowly take another complete breath, and calm your emotions.

Slowly take another complete breath, and focus your mind.

Take another deep breath, and as you exhale feel and see the relationship between your energy and your self.

Take another deep breath, and as you exhale feel and see the relationship between your emotions and your consciousness.

Take another deep breath, and as you exhale feel and see the relationship between your thoughts and your soul.

From your place within the heart, sense the relationship between your personality and your self or soul.

Audibly sound the OM.

Take a deep breath, and slowly return to this time and place.

Namaste.

170

Chapter 16 Commentary

We are blessed to live at a time when we must be mindful of our relationship with substance.

As we've discussed, all consciousness is one. It is born of the relationship of the spirit or purpose with the matter or intelligent activity of the one life. Being born of that relationship, it is the nature of consciousness to relate.

In addition, the consciousness or soul inherits the motivating purpose of spirit. Thus, the characteristics of consciousness include the purpose, power, and will of spirit. These give the soul its direction and motivating impulse.

The soul also inherits the ability of matter to differentiate itself into many, separate forms. Thus, the characteristics of consciousness include the ability to differentiate the one self into many selves.

The one consciousness remains one, but that one has been differentiated into many expressions of the one soul. Each of these expressions has its relationship with the purpose and substance of the one life.

We may say, "my soul," but what we mean is a differentiated portion of *the* soul. Our soul is part of, and has no existence apart from, the soul of the one life. Thus, who and what we are is a fragment of the one life, differentiated from, and eventually reunited with the one life by our identity.

How to Serve Humanity

We may say, "my purpose," but what we mean is a differentiated portion of *the* purpose of the planetary life. Thus, our motivations are part of the motivation of the one life, and we have no purpose apart from that life.

We may say, "my body," but what we mean is a differentiated portion of the matter of the planetary life. Thus, our mind, emotions, and body are part of the substance of the planetary life, and we have no form apart from that life.

Everything we are is part of and exists within the one life.

Chapter 17

Aligning the Personality

Every quality of consciousness relates its portion of planetary matter to spirit. This slowly transforms the self or soul into an identified portion of the one planetary soul.

Thus *consciousness relates matter to spirit.*

Relating our Persona with our Purpose Within the Planetary Life

Sit comfortably, close your eyes, and move into your heart.

Slowly take a complete breath, and relax your body.

Slowly take another complete breath, and calm your emotions.

Slowly take another complete breath, and focus your mind.

Take another deep breath, and as you exhale feel and see the relationship between your energy and your purpose.

Take another deep breath, and as you exhale feel and see the relationship between your emotions and your power.

Take another deep breath, and as you exhale feel and see the relationship between your thoughts and your spirit.

From your place within the heart, sense the relationship between your personality and your place and purpose within the planetary life.

Audibly sound the OM.

Take a deep breath, and slowly return to this time and place.

Namaste.

174

Chapter 17 Commentary

We are blessed to live at a time when the old spiritual paths are no longer adequate and we must transform them and build new ones.

Our heart center alignments begin when we focus in the heart. When we place our consciousness in the heart, we move into and become the state of awareness of the heart. As we've discussed, the heart center awareness is that of universal at-one-ment.

The more we return to and remain in the heart, the more powerful the heart becomes and the more our awareness of at-one-ment grows. The heart becomes increasingly magnetic, a radiant and attractive center of the energy of union.

As we align upward from the heart, through the top of our head, with the one life, we create a permanent alignment of light between our heart and the one planetary life. This vertical alignment becomes a growing channel for the flow of divine purpose, consciousness, and substance.

As we align outward from the heart, to the individuals, groups, and conditions around us, we create channels for the flow of those divine energies out to those people and conditions.

As we align those individuals and groups upward, through the top of their heads, directly to the one life, we create the seeds of their own alignment with the planetary life.

As those we assist experience and respond to the divine energies, they begin to use and develop their own hearts and their alignments with the one life.

And so the creative process continues, for this is how the Law of Relationship is wielded in service to the one planetary life.

Chapter 18

Aligning Planetary Matter and Spirit

Aligning spirit and matter is a natural, normal, every-day activity of your consciousness—it is the Law of Relationship in action.

Your consciousness relates spirit to consciousness, then...

Your consciousness relates spirit to matter, then...

Your consciousness relates matter to consciousness, then...

Your consciousness relates matter to spirit.

It is a simple, creative process that we all perform automatically just by being self aware. Most of humanity performs this process unconsciously, with no real thought, direction, or control.

However, when we become aware that we can choose our state of consciousness, and thus relate a particular portion of the planetary purpose with a particular portion of matter, then we can create consciously, in full waking awareness.

The Magic of Consciousness –
Performing the Law of Relationship

Sit comfortably, close your eyes, take a deep breath and as you inhale move into your heart.

Slowly take a complete breath, and relax your body.

Slowly take another complete breath, and calm your emotions.

Slowly take another complete breath, and focus your mind.

Take another deep breath, and as you inhale feel and see your spiritual purpose flowing into your consciousness.

Inhale another deep breath, and at the moment of stillness following the inhale, feel and see your spiritual purpose flowing from your consciousness into your mind, emotions, and body.

Audibly state the following: 'I dedicate my self to serving the one planetary life. I am that life.'

Take another deep breath, and as you exhale feel and see your body, emotions, and mind aligning with your consciousness.

Take another deep breath, and at the moment of stillness following the exhale, feel and see your body, emotions, and mind aligning with your spiritual purpose.

From your place within the heart, sense the alignment from:

Chapter 18

your purpose to your soul,

your soul to your personality,

your personality to your soul, and

your soul to your spiritual purpose.

Audibly sound the OM.

Take a deep breath, and slowly return to this time and place.

Namaste.

Chapter 18 Commentary

We are blessed to live at a time of alignment.

The method of this new age, by which humanity will re-build its civilization and achieve the realization that we are soul, is alignment. Our preparations for that align-ment, the core of the Law of Relationship in action, are completed in this lesson.

With this technique we receive the final pieces of this alignment. We have learned to focus as the self or soul in the heart, and from the heart to:

Align spirit with consciousness,

Align spirit with matter,

Align matter with consciousness, and

Align matter with spirit.

When used together, in the proper sequence, these be-come the one alignment that is the Law of Relationship in action. They are the basis of the conscious creative process.

That creative process is often divided into four parts, including:

An Ascent,

Union or at-one-ment with the soul,

180

Chapter 18

A Descent, and

Appearance

The four parts of the creative process are analogous to the four parts of a single breath. When focused in the heart:

The exhale is analogous to the ascent,

The momentary pause between an exhale and an inhale is analogous to the stage of Union or at-one-ment,

The inhale is analogous to the Descent, and

The momentary pause between an inhale and an exhale is analogous to the stage of Appearance.

Ascent

The ascent is that portion of the alignment in which the incarnate self aspires toward union with the overshadowing soul. There are a number of ways of doing this, one of which (the method we are using) begins in the heart. From the focus in the heart, we align upward, through the top of the head, with the overshadowing soul or true self, and aspire toward union with the soul.

This process includes relaxing the physical and bio-electric, calming the emotions, and focusing the mind. One becomes relaxed, calm, and focused on the soul.

Union or At-one-ment

This is also known as the height of the meditation, the

How to Serve Humanity

first interlude, and the meditation proper. Union is that
portion of the alignment in which the incarnate self becomes united or at-one with the overshadowing soul.
Once one achieves union, however momentarily, it is
then possible to relate, as soul, with any of the divine
characteristics or qualities that are part of the nature of
the soul. These include those divine energies that pre-
dominate in leadership, teaching, healing, business, the
arts, science, religion, and spirituality.

There are a number of ways of doing this, one of which
(the method we are using) begins in the heart. We will
experience and use a variety of these energies in the
second half of the course.

The spiritual paths and inner disciplines of the last age
tended to focus on and emphasize the Ascent and At-
one-ment process. The Descent and Appearance stages
were often downplayed or ignored.

Descent or Precipitation

The descent is the process whereby the realization or
divine energy contacted during Union is projected
downward. During this portion of the process the divine
is given mental substance, emotional energy, electrical
activity, and finally physical-dense appearance.

Again, there are a number of ways of doing this, each of
which has its advantages and limits. The heart center
focus is one of them. Many would consider heart center
work foundational, and it is true that the heart center
work should be well underway before the mental work is
begun. However, in some ways the higher work of the

heart is more advanced than the highest work of either the intellect or abstract mind.

Appearance or Manifestation

This is also known as the low point of the meditation, and the second interlude. Appearance is that portion of the alignment in which the overshadowing soul precipitates it consciousness and its life into the lower world. Eventually, as a result, the incarnate self becomes united or at one with the overshadowing self, and the outer life becomes a moving picture of the life of the soul. In effect, the difference between the overshadowing spiritual and the mundane material consciousness and life disappears and the two become one.

Again, there are a number of ways of doing this, utilizing different states of consciousness, portions of the instrument, and types of alignment. The heart center is, at the least, a very helpful prelude to the more mental paths.

The spiritual paths and inner disciplines of the Aquarian age tend to focus on and emphasize the Descent and Appearance process. The Ascent and At-one-ment process is included, but as a necessary preparation for the work of Precipitation. This change in emphasis is a result of both the evolution of humanity coming out of the Piscean Age, and of the new Aquarian energies. Where the motion of the Piscean energy was upward toward the divine, the motion of the Aquarian energy is downward from the divine toward the world of affairs. Thus, in this age the emphasis of the path is increasingly moving toward spiritual realization that is practical and immediately applicable in the ordinary life of the seeker.

In order for this conscious creative process to work effectively, both the matter and the activity of the physical, bio-electrical, emotions, and mind must be aligned with and responsive to the soul. Thus, our preparations have included aligning each one of those instruments, and their activities (such as thoughts and emotions) with the soul.

All of the work thus far has been part of the preparation for the practice of the Law of Relationship. In the next two lessons we put the pieces together, and prepare to begin serving humanity in the second half of the course.

Chapter 19

Performing the Creative Process

The conscious creative process is nothing more, or less, than placing oneself in a particular state of consciousness and relating with spirit and matter. As one unites spirit and matter in one's self, that unity is reflected in the outer world. Our daily life and affairs, and the world around us, then reflect the harmony and at-one-ment of the one life.

Utilizing the following techniques, we will help create at-one-ment. We will learn how to recognize the inner misrelationship (between spirit, matter, and consciousness) behind any outer problem, and how to create a solution to that problem via right relationship. We will learn how each and all of us, working together, can help awaken humanity and save Earth.

As the above suggests, awareness *is* response-ability. The more you become aware of *who* you are—of your purpose, place, and function within the planetary life—the more responsible you are for taking your place and performing your function within that life. While you will have the aid and companionship of many who share your purpose, function, and response-ability, the way will not be easy. Most refuse the opportunity many times before accepting the challenge, and awakening to the joy, of the one life. This, also, is part of the path.

If you are ready, then let us begin.

Accepting Your Response-ability

Having completed the basic process for building the creative heart-focused alignment, the next step is to take responsibility for the capacity that alignment gives us:

Sit comfortably, close your eyes, take a deep breath and as you inhale move into your heart.

Slowly take seven deep breaths, and as you exhale relax your body.

Slowly take seven deep breaths, and as you exhale calm your emotions.

Slowly take seven deep breaths, and as you inhale focus your mind.

Take another seven deep breaths, and as you inhale identify as the consciousness in the heart.

As the consciousness in the heart, sense the motion of the breath—in, pause, out, pause (for at least seven full breaths).

Remain still and undisturbed while the breath of the form moves around and through you (for at least 3 minutes).

Audibly state the following: *"I recognize and accept my responsibility to the planetary life."*

Take another seven deep breaths, and as you inhale feel and see your body, emotions, and mind filling with the joy of the one life.

186

Chapter 19

Audibly sound the OM.

Take a deep breath, and as you release it slowly return to this time and place.

Namaste.

How to Serve Humanity

Chapter 19 Commentary

We are blessed to be separate from the one life in which we live, move, and have our being.

As we've seen, our individual identities give us the capacity to move freely within the one life. Up to now we have restricted our motion by our enchantment with thoughts, emotions, and forms. As we liberate our selves from that enchantment, we learn to relate with the one life as part of it.

We learn that the planetary life has a motivating purpose, and that we share in that purpose.

We learn that the planetary life has a consciousness, and that we share in that consciousness.

We learn that the planetary life has embodying matter—mental energy, emotional force, and physical substance—and that we share in that matter.

We learn that in finding our way from separate individuality to the one life, we have gained the capacity to relate any portion of that life—purpose, consciousness, or matter—with any other portion of that life. This is a capacity unique to self aware human beings. Within the entire planetary life, only humanity has this capacity, for it is our function within that life.

We are the planetary organ of conscious creativity. Our purpose and function is to relate the purpose of the one life with its matter, and the matter of the one life with its purpose.

Matter then responds to divine purpose by giving it activity and appearance.

Purpose then responds to divine matter by giving it renewed motivation.

The result is an increasing perfection of the one life.

This is our response-ability as humanity. Each of us shares a small part of that response-ability. Each and all of us can do our part by performing the Law of Relationship.

In the previous lessons we learned how to perform the Law, and having learned how, we are now response-able. We are able to respond to the need of the planetary life by practicing the Law—in our daily life and affairs, and in our work. As we do so, we will help transform ourselves, our lives, and the world around us.

In the next lesson we will outline seven ways of wielding the Law of Relationship, and relate each of those methods with one or more outer professions (such as leader, teacher, healer, artist, etc.). Then, beginning in Lesson 21, we will explore how each of those professions can use the Law as the basis of its contribution to the New World Civilization, heal Earth, and take humanity to the next step in its evolution—self awareness as Soul.

Chapter 20

Taking up Your Place and Function in The Planetary Life

Every outer problem is an expression of a misrelationship within the one life. Humanity is in the unique position to clarify, identify, and resolve those problems by practicing the Law of Relationship. Every member of humanity has a unique potential role to play in this process. Each of us has the ability to perform the Law in our own way, in our own inner lives and outer affairs.

However, for simplicity sake we will divide the practice of the Law into a number of distinct methods or approaches. These methods use the same basic alignment that we developed in the earlier lessons, but they use that alignment to channel a particular portion of the purpose and energy of the planetary life.

Each of these approaches tends to express itself as a particular inner function and through one or more outer professions. In the second half of this work, we will align the purpose and energies of these functions (and some of the related professions).

By the end of the course you will have experienced the inner work of all the basic functions, and will have a foundation for deciding which of them to pursue further as the possible arena of your service to the one life.

Aligning with Our Functions Within the One Life

Having taken responsibility for the capacity of our heart-focused alignment, the next step is to align with the various methods of using that capacity:

Sit comfortably, close your eyes, take a deep breath and as you inhale move into your heart.

Slowly take seven deep breaths, and as you exhale relax your body.

Slowly take seven deep breaths, and as you exhale calm your emotions.

Slowly take seven deep breaths, and as you inhale focus your mind.

Take another seven deep breaths, and as you inhale identify as the consciousness in the heart.

As the consciousness in the heart, sense the motion of the breath—in, pause, out, pause (for at least seven full breaths).

Remain still and undisturbed while the breath of the form moves around and through you.

As it moves, recognize that there are a number of distinguishing motions within the breath of the form.

A portion is the breath or motion of leadership.

Chapter 20

A portion is the breath or motion of education.

A portion is the breath or motion of healing.

A portion is the breath or motion of organization.

A portion is the breath or motion of commerce.

A portion is the breath or motion of art.

A portion is the breath or motion of media.

A portion of the breath or motion of science.

A portion is the breath or motion of religion.

A portion is the breath or motion of spirituality.

Remain still and undisturbed while the one breath, that is many motions, moves around and through you (for at least 3 minutes).

Audibly state the following: "*I recognize the many types of motion within the cyclic breath of the one life.*"

Take another seven deep breaths, and as you inhale feel and see your body, emotions, and mind filling with the joy of the one life.

Audibly sound the "OM."

Take a deep breath, and as you release it slowly return to this time and place.

Namaste.

Chapter 20 Commentary

We are blessed to live at a time when humanity has lost its sense of place and must rediscover its function within the one life.

Up to this point we have focused on the one life as a whole consisting of a positive pole, a negative pole, and a magnetic field of relationship between them. We have explored that whole by focusing as the magnetic field in the heart and aligning from the heart, upward with the positive pole, outward with the negative pole, and upward from the negative pole directly to the positive pole. This is the basic alignment via which one wields the Law of Relationship in service to humanity and the one life.

In the meditations we have aligned the overshadowing purpose of the one life with its embodying substance, and experienced the result in the symbolic breath or motion of form. Matter, including mental energy, emotional force, and etheric substance responds to the impression of purpose by taking on new motions, creating new or transformed thoughts, feelings, and appearance in the world of affairs.

Of course, the few exercises we have performed are only a bare beginning. We are learning how to do the work, and it will take the determined, persistent efforts of all of us to transform the world in which we live.

Chapter 20

As stated before, each of us has a unique role in that transformation, a function as a soul within the one life. Those functions can be described in many ways, but it will help if we begin our exploration of them with general categories or types. Having explained the general types of inner and outer service, and given you some experience with each of them, you will have a basis for deciding which if any of them resonates with or calls to you the most. Having felt the call of a particular type of service, you can then explore that type in greater detail, to discover your particular area of service.

However, we must first decide how we are going to identify and describe those roles.

Since we have worked with the three aspects of purpose, substance, and consciousness, we can look at these types of service as expressions of those three aspects.

Since we have worked with the symbolic motion of substance, we can look at these types of service as types of motion within the breath of the one life.

Since we all live in the world of affairs, we can look at how those motions and expressions can manifest through familiar professions. For instance:

Leadership emphasizes the motion and energy of the first aspect or divine purpose.

Education and Healing emphasize the motion and energy of the second aspect of consciousness.

Organization and Commerce emphasize the motion and energy of the third aspect of substance.

How to Serve Humanity

Other professions, such as Art, Media, Religion, and Spirituality each utilize a particular equation or combination of the motions and energies of the three aspects.

In the following lessons we will explore how the three aspects of divinity, and their motions and energies, can be expressed through each of these professions. This is how we will transform our daily life and affairs: by recognizing the divine within everything we do, connecting with the divine therein, and bringing it into expression via living the Law of Relationship.

Section 3

Performing the Creative Process

How to Serve Humanity

Chapter 21

Leadership

Part 1

When we consciously perform the Law of Relationship, we first focus as the soul, and then trace a triangular alignment up, out, and back up. This triangular alignment remains, no matter which profession one is practicing. What differs are the upper and outer poles of that alignment, its magnetic field, and what flows through it. It is that subtle difference, not their outer appearances, that distinguishes the various professions.

For instance, a leader is someone who is aligned with and has a vision of purpose, and relates that vision to others. The upward alignment is with purpose. That purpose, focused by the consciousness of the leader, produces a vision within their mind. That vision is then aligned outward with those who stand in need of it, and they are then aligned upward directly with that overshadowing purpose.

This is the core of the new type of leadership. Rather than imposing their will, the new type of leader relates the purpose of the one life with a condition, and that condition with the purpose. The resulting at-one-ment unifies motivations (such as values, vision, and mission) at any and all levels of human consciousness and activity, including within their self, their family, their community, and the entire planetary life.

Aligning as a Leader

Having practiced performing the Law of Relationship from a heart-focus, the next step is to perform the Law (in service to humanity and the one life) from each of the new professions. In this first section on Leadership we will take the inner position of a leader. In the second section on Leadership we will perform the alignment as a leader:

Sit comfortably, close your eyes, take a deep breath and as you inhale move into your heart.

Slowly take seven deep breaths, and as you exhale relax your body.

Slowly take seven deep breaths, and as you exhale calm your emotions.

Slowly take seven deep breaths, and as you inhale focus your mind.

Take another seven deep breaths, and as you inhale identify as the consciousness in the heart.

As the consciousness in the heart, align upward, through the top of the head, with the soul of humanity.

Recognize that you are part of the soul of humanity, and as soul have a relationship with the purpose of the planetary life.

As the consciousness in the heart, continue the upward alignment, through the soul of humanity, with the purpose of the one life.

200

Chapter 21

Aligned with that purpose, audibly state the following: "*I receive the divine purpose of the one life in my heart, as it is related to me by my soul. I serve that purpose, accept its power, and do the will of the one life.*" (Remain still and undisturbed, for at least 3 minutes, while divine purpose, power, and will, as stepped down to you by the soul, infuses your heart.)

Audibly sound the "OM."

Take a deep breath, and as you release it slowly relax your attention and return to this time and place.

Namaste.

Chapter 21, Part 1

Commentary

In the previous, Piscean age, the archetypal leader stood at the center of the organization as the source of motivating purpose for that organization. Whether the organization was a family, business, church, community, or nation, the basic alignment used (consciously or unconsciously) was "L" shaped, and could be outlined as follows:

From the leader's point of focus (wherever that was) up to the group purpose,

Back down to the leader's point of focus (bringing whatever portion of that purpose the leader had been able to grasp),

From the leader's point of focus out to the group (radiating whatever portion of that purpose the leader had been able to retain, in whatever form they had been able to envision and express it),

Align the group back to the leader as the source of motivating purpose.

This L shaped alignment was basically the same in any profession or function of the times, whether it was a guru-chela, leader-follower, healer-patient, or whatever. The practitioner was the channel for that particular divine character or quality, and intermediary between it and their client. This was necessarily so, as at the time humanity was not capable of contacting and invoking such energies directly.

There were, however, a number of limits to this old alignment. For instance, it both focused the attention of the group on the persona of the leader, and it fostered dependence on that leader as the source of that purpose, wisdom, or healing.

Fortunately, both humanity and the larger life have changed. The veils between the astral and the physical are dissolving (making the heart center frequencies, among others, much more accessible), and humanity has grown considerably.

These and other changes have made the old L alignment outmoded, and brought in the new triangular alignment.

The new type of leader relates the purpose of a group with a condition (in consciousness and form) of that group, and relates that condition directly to the purpose. This alignment empowers and inspires the members of the group in a way that the old alignment could not. This new triangular alignment can be outlined as follows:

From the leader's point of focus (wherever that is) up to the group purpose,

Back down to the leader's point of focus (bringing whatever portion of that purpose the leader has been able to grasp),

Held in the leader's point of focus, and formulated by the leader into a vision of that purpose.

How to Serve Humanity

From the leader's point of focus out to the group (relating the purpose, via the vision, to the group),

Align the group back up, through the top of their heads, directly with the group purpose (thereby inscribing an alignment from every member of the group to or with that purpose).

This triangular alignment is the basis for every service function that consciously uses the Law of Relationship in this age, including those working in such areas as leadership, teaching, healing, publishing, economy and finance, organization, public relations, etc., etc. The essential difference in the alignment, from one function to another, is the upper point or pole of the alignment, the approach to the lower point or pole of the alignment, and the character of the magnetic field.

In the case of a leader, the upper point will be characterized by divine purpose, power, and will, the magnetic field by motivation or direction, and the negative point by inspiration. The group members will be inspired by the activities of the leader, but (because the alignment directs their attention toward the motivating source rather than the persona of the leader), will not necessarily identify the leader as the source of inspiration.

The new alignment has a number of advantages to the old. It directs the attention of its recipient directly to the source (of purpose, wisdom, healing, etc.) and away from the persona of the leader, teacher, or healer. It inscribes the beginnings of the recipient's own upward alignment, and it thereby creates a direct relationship between the source and the recipient. In the case of leadership, that direct line of relationship becomes the recipient's connection with their own purpose. As that connection with their purpose grows, so does their ability to sense, recognize, and take up their own leadership function.

As the recipients take up their leadership function, they become co-leaders, able to cooperate with each other because they are working directly with and from a shared, unlimited, universal supply of purpose, power, and will.

This new leadership function applies no matter what a practitioner's main area of practice may be. If they are a teacher, healer, entrepreneur, financier, artist, scientist, engineer, pastor, or anything else, they will still have the new relationship with purpose and express it as the new type of leadership.

Thus, the conscious practice of the Law of Relationship will transform leadership.

In Part 1 of Chapter 21 we have explored the identity and work of a leader in the new, Aquarian age. In Part 2 we will explore how to function as a Leader in cooperation with all of those with whom one works.

Chapter 21

Leadership

Part 2

The new type of leader is one who identifies as the soul, aligns their group life with the plan of the one life, and organizes their group to embody that plan. This inner and outer process produces a common inspired vision of truth, and integrates the group around it. As a result, the group members are highly motivated and self directed—individually and collectively.

Having been given at least the beginnings of their own alignment, group members often do not have to be told what to do. They will see a condition within the group life, recognize their relationship with it, and act to resolve that condition without being instructed to do so. At first they will tend to act as individuals, but as the group matures they will increasingly act cooperatively, as an integrated group life.

As the group grows and develops additional points of cooperative leadership arise, all working together to sound the group purpose, clarify its vision, and perform its mission. The purpose of every portion of the group, in relationship with every other portion, then becomes quite clear. Thus aligned through their own purpose with the common purpose, every portion of the group supports every other portion simply by performing its function. The group has then become a one life within the greater life.

Chapter 21

Leading

Having taken the inner position of the leader, in this
second section on Leadership we perform the alignment
as a leader:

Sit comfortably, close your eyes, take a deep breath and
as you inhale move into your heart.

Slowly take seven deep breaths, and as you <u>exhale</u> relax
your body.

Slowly take seven deep breaths, and as you <u>exhale</u> calm
your emotions.

Slowly take seven deep breaths, and as you <u>inhale</u> focus
your mind.

Take another seven deep breaths, and as you <u>inhale</u> identify as the consciousness in the heart.

As the consciousness in the heart, align upward, through
the top of the head, with the soul of humanity.

Recognize that you are part of the soul of humanity, and
as soul have a relationship with the purpose of the planetary life.

As the consciousness in the heart, continue the upward
alignment, through the soul of humanity, with the purpose
of the one life.

Aligned with that purpose, audibly state the following:

"I receive the divine purpose of the one life in my heart, as it is related to me by my soul. I clarify that purpose, and radiate it outward, as inspired motivating vision, to those who share my service to the one life." (Remain still and undisturbed, for at least 3 minutes.)

Audibly sound the *"OM."*

Take a deep breath, and as you release it slowly relax your attention and return to this time and place.

Namaste.

Chapter 21, Part 2

Commentary

The new type of leader is one who identifies as the soul, and as soul aligns with the world of ideas and of meaning. This alignment, as soul with the idea of truth and the meaning of the one life, inspires the leader. It is symbolized in popular imagery by the light bulb that appears above the head at the moment of inspiration or realization.

This image is essentially accurate, as a light does appear above the head at the moment of inspiration, the light of the soul moving down the alignment to the center above the head. This soul light produces in turn a flash of light and moment of realization in the physical brain. The flash of light in the brain produces new pathways, literally new ways of thinking, in the brain.

Thus inspired, the leader is able to inspire others. They do this by aligning with the light above the head, bringing it down into their point of focus in their instrument (such as the heart), and radiating that light outward to those who need it. Those who receive it respond with their own bursts of internal light, and are inspired in turn.

Of course, if this is all that is done those who receive the light would identify the leader as the source. They will have been inspired by the light above the leader's head, as formulated into words and actions by the leader's brain and persona, and (lacking an inspiring upper alignment of their own) will view the leader as the source. If, however, the leader inscribes an upward alignment for them, directly to the source of the alignment, then they will be aligned with that source as the source of ideas, meaning, and inspiration. That higher source will then give direction to their lives, rather than the leader.

This is how the triangular alignment is used in leadership. In the beginning, one must will to form and wield the alignment. One begins with formal meditations, in set times and places, and uses the alignment to relate a portion of the purpose or plan of the one life with a condition in the world of affairs (and that condition with its purpose). As one's ability to wield the alignment grows, one's practice gradually expands to include any moment in which one recognizes a condition that needs aligning. Eventually the alignment is so well developed that it is simply there, permanently functioning, and anyone and any condition that enters one's sphere of influence is automatically aligned with their overshadowing purpose.

As their alignment develops their relationship with purpose increases and they become a more radiant source of motivating purpose, power, and will. In effect, they become a more powerful positive pole. Since the poles must be in balance, their negative pole of substance becomes more powerful as well, and they become more effective in the world of affairs. As the two poles strengthen, the magnetic field grows as well, and the leader becomes more magnetic—both radiatory and attractive.

At the same time, the leader becomes more inspirational. That is, they become an increasing source of inspiration, motivation, and direction for those in their area of influence (family, organization, community, etc.). Since this inspiration is a result of the triangular alignment, those thus inspired increasingly turn to their own alignment with the higher source for ideas, motivation, and direction. This direct alignment strengthens with use, and eventually the followers become leaders in their own right, cooperating with their leader, and each other, in service to the purpose and plan of the one life with which they are all aligned.

The effect of this cooperative response to shared purpose is organic. It is equivalent to the cooperative response of the cells in an organ, such as the heart, to their shared purpose. In order for each of the cells to perform their function, all must work together in coordination, expanding and contracting in sequential rhythm. And the right use of this rhythm is essential.

The meditation alignment, through which one wields the Law of Relationship, follows a regular rhythm. The length of that rhythm will vary depending on the skill of the practitioner and the difficulty of a particular condition. There are four stages to that rhythm, the upward alignment or ascent, the at-one-ment, the precipitation or descent, and appearance. Each of these stages may take moments, or be the main focus of an alignment over a longer cycle such as a day, month, or year. In general, however, the leader will:

Align upward with the overshadowing purpose: While the practitioner (leader, teacher, healer, or whatever) will continue to the next step in the alignment in any case, until the ascent is complete they will treat the next steps as preparatory. It is rather like turning the crank on a hand-powered generator. One keeps turning the crank until enough power is generated to perform the required task. In this case, however, one keeps repeating the meditation cycle until one reaches the place of at-one-ment

At-one with that purpose: The practitioner will continue to perform the triangular alignment, emphasizing at-one-ment with the overshadowing purpose, until this step is finished, and the realization gained is clear and complete. One performs the entire meditation process—ascent, at-one-ment, descent, and appearance—but the emphasis is on at-one-ment. The same pattern of emphasizing the related portion of the meditation cycle is followed at each step of the process.

Descent or Precipitation: Having gained a clear and complete vision of the overshadowing purpose, the practitioner radiates that purpose back down the alignment, giving it shape and form as mental thought, emotional feeling, and etheric activity. When these are fully formulated, they then relate that inspired vision outward to those in their area of influence who need it.

Appearance: When that fully formulated inspired vision of truth is related to those who need it, they respond by inspired action. Those actions, motivated and coordinated by the same clear, complete vision of truth, produce the outer appearance of the overshadowing plan. The alignment back up directly to that plan holds it all together as a continuing, ordered whole.

This is how the leaders of this new Aquarian age lead—through inspired and inspiring vision. The result is a group of cooperative, self-motivated co-leaders, each and all of whom share in that alignment with the divine plan of the one life.

This is how the Law of Relationship is wielded by leaders.

In chapter 22 we will explore how teachers use Divine Love and Wisdom in their practice of the Law of Relationship.

How to Serve Humanity

Chapter 22

Education

The new type of teacher is someone who is aligned with Truth—the reality behind and overshadowing all thought, feeling, activity, and appearance. The teacher uses the primary energy of consciousness, divine love-wisdom, to relate the Truth with a condition in the world of affairs, and to relate that condition with the Truth overshadowing it.

As the overshadowing Truth is related through the student's mind to their brain, their awareness of Truth clarifies. They experience sudden expansions of understanding in which their consciousness grows and their ability to see and act on Truth expands.

When the Truth and matter have been fully aligned, the two become one. The Truth then appears in that condition, in that time and place, and any misrelationships disappear.

This is the way the new type of teacher works. Rather than imposing their realization of Truth, they relate Truth to the student, the student to the Truth, and the student develops their own ability to sense, know, and embody Truth.

Aligning as a Teacher

Having aligned with the energy of purpose and the function of leaders, the next step is to align with the energy of love and the function of teaching. In this first section on teaching we will take the inner position of a teacher. In the second section on teaching we will perform the alignment as a teacher:

Sit comfortably, close your eyes, take a deep breath and as you inhale move into your heart.

Slowly take seven deep breaths, and as you <u>exhale</u> relax your body.

Slowly take seven deep breaths, and as you <u>exhale</u> calm your emotions.

Slowly take seven deep breaths, and as you <u>inhale</u> focus your mind.

Take another seven deep breaths, and as you <u>inhale</u> identify as the consciousness in the heart.

As the consciousness in the heart, align upward, through the top of the head, with the soul of humanity.

Recognize that you are part of the soul of humanity, and as soul have a relationship with the love-wisdom of the planetary life.

As the consciousness in the heart, continue the upward alignment, through the soul of humanity, with the love-wisdom of the one life.

216

Chapter 22

Aligned with that love, audibly state the following:

"I stand receptive to that Love which is my Soul, and Truth is made known to me" (Remain still and undisturbed, for at least 3 minutes, while divine love-wisdom, as stepped down to you by the soul, infuses your heart.)

Audibly sound the *"OM."*

Take a deep breath, and as you release it slowly relax your attention and return to this time and place.

Namaste.

Chapter 22, Part 1

Commentary

In the previous, Piscean age, the archetypal teacher was the source of clarifying Truth for any group. As with leaders, whether the group was a family, business, church, community, or nation, the basic alignment used (consciously or unconsciously) was "L" shaped, and could be outlined as follows:

From the teacher's point of focus (wherever that was) up to the group truth,

Back down to the teacher's point of focus (bringing whatever portion of that truth the teacher had been able to grasp),

From the teacher's point of focus out to the group (radiating whatever portion of that truth the teacher had been able to retain, in whatever form they had been able to envision and express it),

Align the group back to the teacher as the source of clarifying truth.

As discussed in the previous lesson, this L shaped alignment was basically the same in any profession of the times, whether it was a guru-chela, leader-follower, healer-patient, or whatever. The practitioner was the channel for the divine character or quality of their profession, and intermediary between that divine quality and their client. This was necessarily so, as at the time humanity was not capable of contacting and invoking such energies directly.

As noted earlier, both humanity and the larger life have changed, making the old L alignment outmoded, and bringing in the new triangular alignment.

The new type of teacher uses the primary energy of consciousness, divine love-wisdom, to relate a group with the Truth overshadowing them. The teacher relates that Truth with a condition (in consciousness and form) of that group, and relates that condition directly back to the overshadowing portion of Truth. This is the same alignment, the Law of Relationship in action, we have discussed throughout this course.

In this case, the alignment produces flashes of understanding in which the Truth is seen clearly and experienced as a reality. These "aha" moments include literal bursts of light in the brain (in the pre-frontal cortex). These flashes of light (popularly symbolized by a glowing light bulb above the head) create new brain pathways and modes of thinking.

Since these pathways and modes of thinking are produced by the student's own instrument in response to the direct alignment with Truth, they are truly new. In the old method of teaching the teacher in effect gradually copied or grafted their own alignment onto the student. As part of the process, the teacher reproduced their own modes of thinking, feeling, and acting within the instrument of the student. The student was taught the "right way" to think, to feel, and to act. We see this today in, for instance, those physical disciplines (such as

Hatha Yoga or the martial arts) in which students are taught that there is only one correct way to hold a pose or stance, or to perform a motion. And in those disciplines and in those times this was usually quite correct.

This is less often the case today, as the old method has a major limitation that would severely hamper students in these times. While students learned solutions to old problems, they did not learn how to formulate solutions to new conditions which their teachers never faced. Students taught via the old methods do not learn how to think, feel, or act creatively to solve *new* problems.

We see this limitation in thinking in, for instance, college engineering students who were raised in countries where there was always only one right answer to any problem they were given in school. If sent to college in another country, at a school that requires creative thinking to solve new problems that have no one right answer, these engineering students do not know how to respond. They simply have not developed the ability to think creatively to solve new problems.

This type of creative problem solving is not something that can be taught. It cannot be imposed by an external authority. It must be learned by the act of solving new problems for oneself. The new type of teaching nurtures this process by creating the inner conditions under which it is most easily and likely to develop.

The new type of teacher does not offer the right answer (although they may appear to do so). What they are actually doing is offering the means by which the student may realize an answer—in their consciousness, mind, and brain—for themselves.

Chapter 22

As the student develops their alignment, and their solution-realization abilities, they transform their personality from a prison into a vehicle of the soul. The persona becomes an instrument for self realization and the manifestation of Truth.

Along with using the Law of Relationship to inscribe the beginnings of the student's own alignment, the new type of teacher:

Recognizes the student as a soul within the planetary soul, and treats them as such (bringing out the soul within),

Aligns the student with their soul, and their purpose, place, and function as soul within the one life (helping them discover why they are here),

Invokes the student's purpose, place, and function, as soul, into appearance in the world (helping them fulfill their purpose),

Models and gives students the tools for becoming the soul in the world of affairs.

Thus, the conscious practice of the Law of Relationship is transforming teaching.

In Part 1 of Chapter 22 we have explored the identity and work of a Teacher in the new, Aquarian age. In Part 2 we will explore how to function as a Teacher in cooperation with all of those with whom one works.

Chapter 22

Teaching

Part 2

The new teacher focuses on using their alignment to build the student's alignment. They use their alignment as teacher's to inscribe the beginnings of an alignment in their students, and then support their student's efforts to continue building their own alignment.

The teacher performs their inner work whenever they recognize the need for it, taking that recognition of need as an indication of relationship with the solution. They then perform their inner work, usually quietly and behind the scenes. Often those who benefit from the teacher's efforts do not realize that anything has been done for them. They may have no basis for understanding it, no need to know, or may even misunderstand and object if they learned about it.

Thus, for the most part, the teacher performs their work without any outer recognition or reward, simply doing what needs to be done to assist those who present themselves for teaching.

Chapter 22

Acting as a Teacher

Having taken the inner position of a teacher, in this second section on teaching we will perform the alignment as a teacher:

Sit comfortably, close your eyes, take a deep breath and as you inhale move into your heart.

Slowly take seven deep breaths, and as you exhale relax your body.

Slowly take seven deep breaths, and as you exhale calm your emotions.

Slowly take seven deep breaths, and as you inhale focus your mind.

Take another seven deep breaths, and as you inhale identify as the consciousness in the heart.

As the consciousness in the heart, align upward, through the top of the head, to and through the soul of humanity, with that divine love-wisdom that reveals Truth.

Aligned through the soul of humanity, with the love-wisdom of the one life, invoke the Truth downward, into your heart, by audibly stating the following:

"Standing midway between humanity and the Truth, wielding the love of the Soul, I invoke the overshadowing Truth into my heart, and project that Truth outward with that wisdom that produces understanding." (Remain still and undisturbed, for at least 3 minutes.)

Draw a line of light upward, from the physical brain of humanity directly to the overshadowing Truth. (Pause for at least 1 minute.)

Audibly sound the *"OM."*

Take a deep breath, and as you release it slowly relax your attention and return to this time and place.

Namaste.

Chapter 22, Part 2

Commentary

The teacher can only *appear* to tell the Truth because the truth cannot be put into words. The best that can be done is to create a representation of truth, and thus teachers of the old school taught via symbol and allegory. These are still used, but the new teacher also uses the triangular alignment.

Since the soul is born of the relationship between spirit and matter, its primary energy, divine love-wisdom, brings the capacity to both see and understand relationships.

That ability to see or experience the relationship of everything within the one life we call divine love.

The capacity to understand those relationships we call wisdom.

Love without wisdom is foolish. Wisdom without love is empty. Thus, love and wisdom are two aspects or poles of a single energy, and we call that energy divine love-wisdom.

The primary work of the new teacher is to relate Truth to the student in a manner that produces understanding. This is done by relating the student with the Truth, using love-wisdom, through the triangular alignment.

The teacher performs this process by:

Taking a midway point of focus between their student group and the Truth overshadowing them (depending on the students, in the heart or head),

Aligning upward with that portion of the Truth (via a line of light, through the top of the head),

At-oneing with that portion of Truth (as Soul),

Bringing that realized portion of Truth downward through their mind into their brain (along the line of light),

Projecting that Truth outward (along a line of light) as thought and feeling, and expressing it in word and action (via tone, content, and quality),

Aligning that student group upward, from the students' physical brains, directly to the overshadowing portion of Truth (via a line of light),

Leaving that alignment in place, the teacher relaxes their attention.

In this context "understanding" literally means to "stand under." It refers to the alignment the teacher helps build for the student, from the student's brain, through their mind, with the overshadowing Truth.

The result is a student who has a direct relationship with and experience-based understanding of Truth. In this case, "Truth" refers to that overshadowing reality that is above the physical, vital, emotional, and mental realms. It is the undistorted idea that is the source of thought, feeling, and appearance.

Chapter 22

As an example, imagine that while you are out in your front yard one of the neighborhood children, a four-year-old girl, shows you a tiny new action figure. During her excited description of this figure she tells you that she knows the doll is a girl because the face is "cute."

"Is a pretty face the only difference between boys and girls?" you ask.

Frowning in puzzlement, she replies, "I don't know."

This little girl has just given voice to an illusion—the distorted thought that what makes girls different from boys is that girls have cute faces while boys do not. At this point, that may be just about all she knows, making it part of the foundation of her gender identity. This is a beginning, at four years old, of a distorted idea of femininity. If left unchecked, this distortion can lead to an unending quest for the unachievable—a perfect, female appearance.

The fact that you recognize the seeds of that condition in that little girl indicates that you are in a position of relationship between that little girl and the solution to her condition. You are in the position to relate her with the Truth.

Although she is only four, has not yet developed the ability to understand what you might tell her, and you are not in a parental relationship with her, the fact that you see her condition and can relate her with the solution makes it your responsibility to do so. Her soul created the karmic circumstances that placed her before you, and it is up to your soul to respond.

Recognizing this, you focus in the heart, align upward with that portion of the Truth which is the idea of the divine feminine, align the idea of the divine feminine down and out to the little girl, and up from the little girl's brain directly to the overshadowing idea.

Holding that alignment, you say, "There is a great deal more to girls than a pretty face."

Then you drop the subject, and move the conversation on to other topics until she scampers off to resume her play.

You have planted a seed, and drawn the beginning of a line of light that will nourish that seed. In the coming weeks, months, and years you renew and strengthen that alignment, building toward the point where the little girl, who has now become a woman, is ready to take up that inner work on her own.

This inner work was done for you, by a teacher. Those who become teachers do it for others, in turn, for this is the true inner work of the teacher. This, also, is the Law of Relationship in action.

In chapter 23 we will explore how healers use Divine Love and Wisdom in their practice of the Law of Relationship.

Chapter 23

Healing

Part 1

The new type of healer is an advocate of right relationship—they bring that which is out of alignment with the one life, back into alignment, using the Law of Relationship.

All conditions of dis-ease are expressions of mis-relationship between various portions of the one life. When an individual for instance, formulates and acts on their own plans (apart from those of the one life), their actions inevitably produce disharmony within that life. If the individual persists, that disharmony will eventually manifest as a condition of disease.

The healer uses the primary energy of consciousness, divine love-wisdom, to establish right relationship between that separated consciousness and the one life. That right relationship brings their individual inner and outer life back into alignment with the one life. The resulting harmony manifests as health, and any condition of disease disappears.

This is the way the new type of healer works.

Aligning as a Healer

Having aligned with the energy and function of teachers, the next step is to align with the energy and function of healing. In this first section on healing we will take the inner position of a healer. In the second section on healing we will perform the alignment as a healer:

Sit comfortably, close your eyes, take a deep breath and as you inhale move into your heart.

Perform the usual opening alignment—relaxing your physical body, calming your emotions, focusing your mind, and identifying as the consciousness in the heart.

As the consciousness in the heart, align upward, through the top of the head, with the soul of humanity.

Recognize that you are part of the soul of humanity, and as soul have a relationship with the planetary life.

As the consciousness in the heart, continue the upward alignment, through the soul of humanity, with the love-wisdom of the one life.

Aligned with that love, audibly state the following:

"I stand receptive to that Love which is the Soul, and know the relationship of the one with the whole."

(Remain still and undisturbed, for at least 3 minutes, while divine love-wisdom, as stepped down to you by the soul, infuses your heart.)

230

Chapter 23

Audibly sound the *"OM."*

Take a deep breath, and as you release it slowly relax your attention and return to this time and place.

Namaste.

Chapter 23, Part 1

Commentary

The Piscean Age Healer

The Piscean age healer was and is an advocate for an ideal—usually an ideal form. This is hardly surprising, given that the predominant energy of the age was the Sixth Ray of Aspiration to an Ideal, and much of the work of that age was quite properly focused on building the forms of civilization.

Much good was accomplished during that age, including creating a world-wide civilization and economy, and the ideal of a perfected instrument of the soul.

During the Piscean age, the ideal purpose of the healer was to help the soul produce ever-more-effective instruments (mental, emotional, vital, and physical). This motive directed and informed the work of all healers who were aligned with the one life.

However, with the movement into Aquarius the motivating purpose changed, and the old methods are ceasing to be effective. Healers are having to change with the age if they are to continue to follow their calling.

The Aquarian Age Healer

As mentioned above, the new Aquarian healer is an

advocate of right relationship. They use the Law of Relationship to bring the incarnate consciousness, and its forms, back into alignment with the one life. This is true whether they are working with the physical-dense, vital, emotional, or mental instrument, or whether they are working with individuals, groups, communities, or nations.

In any case, the conditions of disease they work with will be expressions of mis-relationship between various portions of the one life. When a nation, for instance, formulates and acts on its own plans (apart from those of the one life), its actions inevitably produce disharmony within that life. If the nation persists, that disharmony will eventually manifest as a condition or conditions of disease.

We see this today in the common misrelationship between America's children and abundant supply. The rate of overweight and obese children has exploded, bringing with it a severe rise in diabetes, asthma, allergies, and a host of other diseases.

The root of this problem is not the overabundance itself, or even the quality of the supply of food and entertainment. These are symptoms of a misrelationship with purpose. America's children are out of alignment with their purpose, and because of this they lack motivation and direction.

Because of this lack of motivation, the children turn to foods that are empty of vitality, and entertainments that lack meaning or quality, simply for the stimulation they provide.

So long as this misrelationship continues, so long as the

children are adrift without a vision of purpose within and relationship to the greater life, their condition of disease will continue to worsen. Simply educating them and their parents in nutritional diets and the need for physical activity will not bring healing. Their life must be given meaning and direction.

The new healer uses the primary energy of consciousness, divine love-wisdom, to establish right relationship between the misaligned, separated consciousness and the one life. That right relationship brings the separated inner and outer life back into alignment with the one life. The resulting harmony manifests as health, and any condition of disease disappears.

This is the way the new type of healer works.

For America's youth, this would begin with an alignment with purpose, including: the purpose of America within the planetary life, of their community within America, of their family within their community, and of themselves within their family. As this alignment with purpose is established, it would become the source of motivation and direction in their lives, influencing every thought, feeling, and action.

They would remain individuals, growing children, but children who are motivated and inspired by a sense of purpose.

Of course, this cannot be accomplished by attempting to heal the children alone. It can only be done by healing the entire planetary life. Thus, there are those healers who focus their efforts on every portion of that life, including those who specialize in working with the physical,

Chapter 23

vital, emotional, and mental bodies of individuals, families, communities, and nations.

Many of these healers might not be recognized as healers, as they work outside the boundaries of what most consider healing. For instance, healers who align a nation with its purpose might be found in an occupation normally associated with leadership. However, as we discussed in Lesson 21, a leader uses the alignment to wield the energy of purpose.

If someone in the outer position of a leader specializes in using the energy of love-wisdom, via the alignment, to produce right-relationship, then they are a healer.

One's outer occupation or profession is a label for what you do in the world of affairs. It does not describe who you are as soul.

Every soul has a particular relationship with the purpose and substance of the one life. That relationship includes its particular predominant divine energy.

A soul whose predominant energy is divine purpose is primarily a leader.

A soul whose predominant energy is divine love-wisdom is primarily a teacher or healer.

The same is true of the other soul functions we will cover in the following lessons.

A healer is a healer because their soul is that of a healer. This remains true no matter what their outer occupation may be. Their natural tendency, as soul, is to use divine love-wisdom to realign conditions of misrelationship. This is who they are.

In Part 1 of Chapter 23 we have explored the identity and work of a healer in the new, Aquarian age. In Part 2 we will explore how to function as a healer in cooperation with all of those with whom one works.

Chapter 23

Healer

Part 2

The new healer uses their alignment to bring their patients back into right relationship with the one life. They relate their patient's embodied condition of misrelationship with its overshadowing solution, and relate that overshadowing condition of right relationship with their patient. As the embodied condition and the overshadowing solution become one, their patient is healed.

Often, the patient will not accept the fact of healing unless they receive it with an outer activity that they recognize as a method of healing. In those cases, the healer uses whatever outer activity is most acceptable to the patient. However, in all cases the outer activity is merely a means of delivering the realization of healing. The true method of healing is the inner work.

The healer performs their inner work whenever they recognize the need for it, taking that recognition of need as an indication of relationship with the condition. They then perform their inner work, usually quietly and behind the scenes. Often those who benefit from the healer's efforts do not realize that anything has been done for them. They may have no basis for understanding it, no need to know, or may even misunderstand and object if they learned about it.

Thus, for the most part, the healer performs their work without any outer recognition or reward, simply doing what needs to be done to assist those who present themselves for healing.

Chapter 23

Acting as a Healer

Having taken the inner position of a healer, in this second section on healing we will perform the alignment as a healer:

When you recognize a condition of dis-ease, take a deep breath and as you inhale move into the heart and identify as the consciousness in the heart.

As the consciousness in the heart, recognize that that condition is the outer expression of a mis-relationship with the one life.

Align upward, through the top of the head, to and through the soul of humanity, with that love-wisdom that is divine relationship.

Invoke the consciousness and energy of divine relationship into your heart by silently sounding the *OM*.

As the consciousness in the heart, resonating with right relationship, align upward, through the top of the head, with that divine purpose overshadowing that outer condition.

As the consciousness in the heart, resonating with right relationship and aligned with the overshadowing divine purpose, align outward with that condition of mis-relationship.

Project that overshadowing purpose to that condition by audibly stating the following:

"Standing midway between this condition and its divine purpose, I project right relationship outward with that love that produces healing." (Remain still and undisturbed, for at least 3 minutes.)

Draw a line of light upward, from the physical brain of the portion of humanity involved, directly to the overshadowing purpose of that condition. (Pause for at least 1 minute.)

Sound the *"OM"* (audibly or silently, depending on the outer situation).

Take a deep breath, and as you release it slowly relax your attention and return to this time and place.

Namaste.

Chapter 23, Part 2

Commentary

The Aquarian healer uses the Law of Relationship to bring their patients back into right relationship with the one life. When they observe a condition of misrelationship in the world around them, whether presented in an individual or a group, they:

Recognize that they have a relationship with that condition, or they would not have been presented with it,

Recognize that they have a response-ability for that condition, to those who are suffering from it, and for the divine purpose overshadowing it,

Identify as their self or soul, which is a healer, part of the healing consciousness of the one life,

Align upward with the overshadowing purpose of and solution to that condition,

Align outward with that condition, invoke the solution, and project it outward to that condition.

Relate those suffering from that condition back upward, directly to the overshadowing solution.

Hold the solution and the condition in right relationship, via this alignment, until the two become one.

Every embodied condition of misrelationship has an

overshadowing solution. We know this because of the Law of Relationship. Remember, whenever and wherever there is a positive pole, there must be an equally strong negative pole. The fact that a "negative" condition of misrelationship exists indicates that a "positive" solution of right relationship exists as well. The work of the healer consists of using the energy of Love, as the soul, to bring the two poles together into one. At that point, the embodied condition becomes that of right relationship, and the illness disappears.

This is how the healer practices the Law of Relationship.

The knowledge that conditions of disease are produced by misrelationships can itself be a source of misrelationship. For instance, there is a tendency to blame those who suffer from a disease for causing their disease. This tendency is based on a misunderstanding of the source of the misrelationship.

A condition of misrelationship is never limited to an individual. It always arises within a portion of humanity. If that condition of misrelationship persists, then it will eventually outpicture as disease within that portion. Not every member of the group will get sick, and the specific disease will differ from one member to another depending on additional factors.

Take for instance misrelationships with food. There are many types of misrelationships with food within humanity. At first they are relatively minor, producing nothing more serious than a gradual weight gain, or cycles of weight loss and gain. However, if the inner cause is left untreated and allowed to grow, it can eventually produce a wide variety of outer conditions of disease.

Chapter 23

The most common include binge eating disorder, Bulimia nervosa, and Anorexia nervosa. While these examples are expressed through distinctive behaviors (rather than bacteria or viruses), that merely makes it easier to discover their true cause. The question, "Why do they have these symptoms?" leads from the outer behavior to the underlying emotional condition.

In every case, the emotional conditions producing these illnesses are themselves caused by a thought. That thought, for instance, may be, "People have no value unless (they are thin, young, beautiful, rich...)." However, thoughts such as these are distortions. They are out of relationship with the one life and produce disharmony in those who are caught up by them.

Every human being is equal in potential, equally part of the one life, equal in value to that life. Thus, any thought-form that qualifies or places a condition on the value of human beings is in misrelationship with the one life, and will (if harbored and fed) produce a condition of disease.

Such thoughts are never ours alone, but are shared with vast portions of humanity. Within those portions, particularly among those who become caught up by a particular thought, they begin to control our emotions and through our emotions our behavior and experience. The resulting behavior can produce experiences that carry extreme emotional trauma. This trauma can in turn produce the behaviors typical of a particular disease. Thus:

Distorted thoughts produce distorted emotions,

Distorted emotions create and attract distorted

243

behavior and experiences,

Distorted experiences produce emotional trauma,

Emotional trauma produces distorted behavior (the outer disease).

This is, of course, an oversimplification. But the basic outline is correct.

A point that needs to be added here is that a trauma suffered by one person (person A) can result in behavior that produces trauma in another person (person B), that results in another type of behavior. As an extreme example, you have a boy, who was abused by a parent as a child, growing up to be an abuser. The abused boy abuses their own child, who grows up as a victim—not necessarily becoming an abuser themselves, but becoming someone who is unable to trust, because their trust was abused as a child. Someone who is unable to commit to relationships, whatever the specific symptoms may be.

In bacterial or viral diseases, the question, "Why do they have these symptoms?" traditionally leads to the bacterial or viral invader. The form-oriented healer tends to stop there, having found a cause they can see and appreciate. The new Aquarian healer looks beyond the bacterium or virus to the subtle misrelationship that caused it to run amuck.

Again, behind the apparent outer cause will be found an emotional condition, and behind that a distorted thought. The Aquarian healer includes the outer condition, the distorted emotion, and the distorted thought in

244

their alignment, recognizes them as part of a single condition of misrelationship, and adjusts them all via the practice of the Law of Relationship.

Another point that really needs to be made is that you have *societal* conditions of mis-relationship. When I was young, children were sent outside to play. "Go outside and play." was a very common command. If you did something wrong, you were sent outside. If the parents wanted some time alone, you were sent outside. The outdoors was considered a healthy place for children to be; and it got them out of the way so that adults had time of their own—to relax and recuperate from being a parent, from the work day, whatever it was.

Now, when children are sent someplace they are more often sent to their room. Playing outside is considered much more dangerous than it used to be, and when they do play outside children are often made to wear safety equipment such as helmets, and elbow and knee pads. As a result, children now spend an inordinate amount of time indoors, watching some type of screen—video games, television, internet, etc.—and less and less time outside, running around, playing in the dirt, eating sand, climbing trees, skinning their knees, all the outdoor activities children got into.

As the result, children's immune systems are not being challenged anything like the way they used to be—at least not in North America. As a result, their busy young immune systems are not being given enough to do, and wind up looking for something. Sometimes their immune system finds a foreign substance that it decides is toxic, but which really isn't. And so you have a host of allergies developing in young children today, basically because the indoor environments where they spend their time are too clean. It turns out that running around outdoors, playing in the dirt, and climbing trees really is good for children.

The diseases that result from too much time indoors are due to societal conditions. It's not just the individual karma of the child that has that specific disease. It's also karma resulting from a condition within the entire culture. Yes, there is a relationship between that child, as a Soul, and the societal karma in which they incarnate. But it is not that child's fault that they have that disease. It is a shared responsibility of that entire culture. And this is increasingly becoming the case, with conditions of disease, as humanity becomes more group aware—more aware of our self as part of the human kingdom.

The healer performs their inner work whenever they recognize the need for it, taking that recognition of need as an indication of relationship with the condition. They then perform their inner work, usually quietly and behind the scenes. Often those who benefit from the healer's efforts do not realize that anything has been done for them. They may have no basis for understanding it, no need to know, or may even misunderstand and object if they learned about it.

Thus, for the most part, the healer performs their work without any outer recognition or reward, simply doing what needs to be done to assist those who present themselves for healing.

What is recognized is the outer activity the healer performs. For instance, an Aquarian healer will often get a certification in some recognized outer form of healing—becoming a doctor, a physician's assistant, a nurse, an acupuncturist, a naturopath, a chiropractor, whatever fits for them—and will perform that as their outer activity, while performing the inner alignment (the inner practice of right relationship that is the true healing) behind the scenes.

We have all presented ourselves for healing, and been healed, in this manner. Those who become healers do it for others, in turn, for this is the true inner work of the healer. This, also, is the Law of Relationship in action.

In chapter 24 we will explore how the organizers of the Aquarian age use Divine Order in their practice of the Law of Relationship.

How to Serve Humanity

Chapter 24

Organization

Part 1

The new type of organizer is an advocate of divine law and order—they precipitate divine purpose into the mental, emotional, and vital realms using the magic of consciousness.

All conditions of disorganization are expressions of mis-relationship between substance and purpose. That over-shadowing purpose may be unclear, poorly stated, or misinterpreted. When a group, for instance, formulates and acts on their own plan, their organized activities inevitably produce disorder within the one life. If the organization persists in their actions, that disorder will eventually manifest as conflict within the one life.

The Aquarian organizer uses the Law of Relationship to move divine intent into appearance. Substance responds by re-ordering itself into a moving picture of that divine purpose. When a group uses the creative process in this way, their organized activities inevitably produce order within the one life.

This is the way the new type of organizer works.

Aligning as an Organizer

Having aligned with the energy and function of healers, the next step is to align with the energy and function of organizing. In this first section on organizing we will take the inner position of an organizer. In the second section on organizing we will perform the alignment as an organizer:

Sit comfortably, close your eyes, take a deep breath and as you inhale move into your heart.

Perform the usual opening alignment—relaxing your physical body, calming your emotions, focusing your mind, and identifying as the consciousness in the heart.

As the consciousness in the heart, align upward, through the top of the head, with the soul of humanity.

Recognize that you are part of the soul of humanity, and as soul have a relationship with the planetary life.

As the consciousness in the heart, continue the upward alignment, through the soul of humanity, with the law and order of the one life.

Aligned with that order, audibly state the following:

"I stand receptive to the precipitating purpose of the one life, from the overshadowing spiritual soul, into my consciousness and into the substantial forces of my bodies via my heart."

(Remain still and undisturbed, for at least 3 minutes,

Chapter 24

while divine love-wisdom, as stepped down to you by the soul, infuses your heart.)

Audibly sound the *"OM."*

Take a deep breath, and as you release it slowly relax your attention and return to this time and place.

Namaste.

Chapter 24, Part 1

Commentary

Organization in the Aquarian age is so different from that of the Piscean that until recently Aquarian organizations were often not recognized as organizations. People simply did not see them. It wasn't the observers fault. Their persona simply had not been through the experiences that would enable them to recognize the new type of organization as an organization. This is another example of the old and new alignments in action.

The old type of organization, with which we are all so familiar, is built with the Law of Relationship, using the "L" shaped alignment. Typically, the leader at the center aligns upward with the group purpose, focuses that purpose, and pronounces it to the group personnel. The group then responds with that intelligent activity which we identify as the organization.

In such an organization:

The end in form is known from the beginning,

The goal is seen as an ideal form,

That ideal form unfolds in a sequential—1–2–3–4— manner,

The structure is centralized,

Power flows from the center, outward, and

Chapter 24

Success is evaluated in numerical terms.

A good example of this is seen in the old type of business. One of the first things one does when starting the old type of business is formulate a Business Plan. That plan will indicate what the goal of the business is (in numerical terms), and lay out the sequence of activities that will achieve that goal, and the power structure that will direct those activities.

A Business Plan may, for instance, indicate that the goal is to be the #1 bottling company west of the Mississippi, grossing $250 million annually, in 15 years. That Business Plan would be one of the first things requested by a bank or venture capitalist when applying for a start-up loan.

There is nothing inherently wrong with any of this. If the motivating purpose was in alignment with divine intent, and the leader kept the organization focused on and aligned with that purpose, then the result would have been in right relationship with the one life. Variations of this process were used throughout the Piscean age, and produced the world-wide civilization in which we live and from which we derive so many benefits. However, its time, its age, has passed, and the old methods are ceasing to work.

There is no need to examine the difficulties with this type of organizational alignment and structure as we are already quite familiar with them. We will simply add that the energies of the new Aquarian age cannot flow through this old alignment or through the structure created by this alignment. Thus, in order to perform the work of the Aquarian age as organized groups, an entirely new alignment and structure are needed.

The new type of Aquarian organization is, of course, built with the Law of Relationship, using the triangular alignment. In this new type of organization:

The end in consciousness is known from the beginning,

The purpose is seen as the conscious precipitation of divine intent,

That intent unfolds in a non-sequential manner,

The structure is synthetic, and non-centralized,

Power flows from above directly to the entire group, and

Progress is determined by the manifestation of the group intent.

The old style organization is a physical form, and thus its life is limited to the cycle of the form. Every form is born, matures, declines, and passes away. Thus, all Piscean style organizations must eventually die. This is not true of the Aquarian organization.

The new Aquarian organization is essentially a creative activity of the collective consciousness of its members. Thus, the life cycle of that organization is not determined by its form, but by that creative focus. So long as the members of the organization maintain the triangular alignment between the overshadowing purpose and the embodying mental energy, emotional force, and vital substance, then the organization will continue.

When the group purpose is fully in appearance, the

organization has served its purpose and the alignment is withdrawn. The organization then quietly dissolves, in right relationship with the one life.

This is possible because the organizers have remained identified with the creative process throughout the life of the organization. That process works something like this:

Seeing a Need

At some point, a group within the one life perceives a need and a purpose within the planetary life. This group sees that need and purpose because they have a soular relationship with it. Some may perceive the outer condition first, while others see the overshadowing purpose, but in either case the one reveals the other.

Some of the members of this group describe that condition and begin calling on others for assistance.

Invoking Purpose

At this point, the group invokes divine purpose, power, and will, even if they are not leaders (except in the sense that we all are, as the energy of leadership is part of every soul). That energy of leadership focuses and clarifies the purpose of the group, and motivates them to embody that purpose.

Invoking Wisdom

As additional members appear (each with their own abilities and potential) the group begins to take up its work. At this point the group invokes divine love/wisdom, even if they are not healers or teachers (except in the sense that we all are, as the energy of healing/teaching is part of every soul). That energy of teaching produces understanding of the group purpose.

Invoking Order

As the group grows in clarity and understanding, it begins to invoke divine law and order. This is the primary energy of the new type of organization. It can be described as the energy of magic, and is the primary energy used in the creative process itself. All Aquarian organizers have this energy predominating somewhere in their persona and/or soul. It is part of what makes them the new type of organizer.

As that divine law and order is invoked downward, it brings the overshadowing purpose with it. In a sense, this is what divine law and order is—divine purpose moving downward via magic—in this case, the magic of consciousness.

As that divine law and order moves downward it orders the mental energy, emotional force, and vital substance of that condition.

The mental energy becomes the thought-forms of the solution to that condition.

The emotional energy becomes the force that will move those thoughts into activity.

The vital substance becomes those thoughts in activity—the underlying pattern of the outer form.

The outer form of the solution then appears, as a moving picture of that vital activity.

Chapter 24

This outer form is not the solution, but a reflection of the solution. The solution to the condition is the ordered energy, force, and substance, which is made available to humanity through that outer form. You could say the form is the package that contains the solution.

Recognizing this, the Aquarian organizer remains focused on the inner creative process, and not on the outer appearance. They recognize the outer form of the organization, and of their role in it, as convenient appearances. Thus, when it comes time for them to move into another outer role, they do so without regret or triumph (no matter the nature of that role). And when the outer organization has served its purpose, they dissolve it without concern, releasing the substance involved to its next task as they turn to theirs.

In Part 1 of Chapter 24 we have explored the identity and work of an organizer in the new, Aquarian age. In Part 2 we will explore how to function as an organizer in cooperation with all of those with whom one works.

Chapter 24

Organizer

Part 2

The new organizer uses their alignment to create order out of disorder. The type of order with which they work is the divine order of the soul, not the organization of the form. From their perspective, misrelationships between divine purpose and substance produce disorder within consciousness.

This disorder of the consciousness is not related to the degree of organization of the form. The form always responds to a focus of intent by organizing itself into an intelligent activity. It does so whether or not that intent is selfish or divine. Thus, the fact of being well organized in the outer world is not related to the degree of right relationship within the consciousness.

The consciousness is ordered by the activity of relating divine purpose with substance, and divine substance with purpose. As the soul is ordered by this practice of the Law of Relationship, that inner order is reflected into the mental, emotional, vital, and physical realms.

Chapter 24

Acting as an Organizer

Having taken the inner position of a organizer, in this second section on organization we will perform the alignment as an organizer:

When you recognize a condition of disorder, take a deep breath and as you inhale move into the heart and identify as the consciousness in the heart.

As the consciousness in the heart, recognize that that condition is the outer expression of a mis-relationship with the one life.

Align upward, through the top of the head, to and through the soul of humanity, with divine law and order.

Invoke the consciousness and energy of divine order into your heart by silently sounding the *OM*.

As the consciousness in the heart, resonating with divine order, align upward, through the top of the head, with that divine purpose overshadowing that outer condition.

As the consciousness in the heart, resonating with divine order and aligned with the overshadowing divine purpose, align outward with that condition of mis-relationship.

Project that overshadowing purpose to that condition by audibly stating the following:

"I stand receptive to the precipitating purpose of the one life, from the overshadowing spiritual soul of humanity, through my soul, and into the substantial forces of this condition via my heart." (Remain still and undisturbed, for

at least 3 minutes.)

Draw a line of light upward, from the physical brain of the portion of humanity involved, directly to the overshadowing purpose of that condition. (Pause for at least 1 minute.)

Sound the *"OM"* (audibly or silently, depending on the outer situation).

Take a deep breath, and as you release it slowly relax your attention and return to this time and place.

Namaste.

Chapter 24, Part 2

Commentary

The new organizer is quite similar in their methods to the other new professions we've discussed. Like them, the organizer wields the Law of Relationship via a triangular alignment of the consciousness. That alignment is their primary method of performing their work. However, for the organizer the alignment is more than a method. It is the actual goal.

This concept is still a bit abstract at this point in the Aquarian age, but the following may help.

In the Piscean age the goal of the organizer was to organize matter. This is seen in the characteristics of the Piscean organization outlined in Part 1:

The end in form is known from the beginning,

The goal is seen as an ideal form,

That ideal form unfolds in a sequential—1–2–3–4—manner,

The structure is centralized,

Power flows from the center, outward, and

Success is evaluated in numerical terms.

In the Aquarian age the goal of the organizer is to

order consciousness. This is seen in the characteristics of the Aquarian organization outlined in Part 1:

The purpose is seen as the conscious precipitation of divine intent,

That intent unfolds in a non-sequential manner,

The structure is synthetic, and non-centralized,

Power flows from above directly to the entire group, and

Progress is determined by the manifestation of the group intent.

In the Piscean age, organizers were working to create the physical structures and institutions of the old civilization. Their organizational activities were directed outward onto form.

In the Aquarian age, organizers are working to create the inner alignments and practices of the new state of consciousness. Their organizational activities are directed inward to the soul.

Let me give you a simple example of what I mean:

Recently I was working on the text of a lesson when I heard a child cry "Help!" Next thing I knew I was headed out our front door.

We live on a street of modest, well-cared-for homes with small yards. In Phoenix, yards are more often covered with gravel and decorated with cactus rather than grass, and as a result the local children use the street as their main playground.

Chapter 24

Of the ten homes on our block, four have young children, making it a very busy street. I've seen bicycle races, battles between Darth Vader and Luke Skywalker, countless games of hide-and-seek, tag, and even a snowball fight (using snow trucked in from the local mountains, in the back of a childless neighbor's pickup truck, for the purpose).

The street itself carries hints of all this, as broken bits of toys are left behind by the tides of play—the propeller from a toy airplane, a piece of the handle of a light saber, the head of a tiny doll. Too small for adults to bother picking up, most will be washed away by the street sweeper, only to be replaced by subsequent tides.

On that afternoon it was the hour after the children returned from school, but before the adults returned from work. So when I heard a child cry "Help!" I rushed outside knowing that I might be the nearest adult.

A boy was standing on the sidewalk in front of our house, bent over, arms stretched out and down, with his coat pulled over his head.

"Billie?" I called as I hurried up.

"The zipper's stuck in my hair," Billie replied.

Taking a close look I saw that Billie was well and truly trapped. The zipper must have been stuck. He'd tried to remove the coat by pulling it over his head, only to have the zipper grab the hair on the top of his head halfway through the process. He couldn't see, and couldn't move without pulling on his hair.

I moved into my heart, and said, "Hang on, I'll have you free in a minute."

I aligned from my heart with Billie's emotional body, to help keep him calm, and then moved part of my awareness into my ajna so I could assess the situation. I contemplated the scissors in the Swiss Army Knife in my pocket, but decided to try that last as if I cut Billie's hair I'd have to explain why to his mom.

Holding the alignment from my heart with Billie, and with my ajna, I reached out. "Let's see if I can free it," I said.

Gripping his hair firmly, between the jacket and his head, I carefully worked the hair free, a few strands at a time. Once free, and jacket off, Billie thanked me and went on his way.

This story illustrates several important things about the new type of organization.

It began with an inner alignment of the consciousness.

The precise alignment was determined by the situation.

I focused as the soul in the heart in order to have the right quality of consciousness for the person I was working with.

I aligned with him in order to calm him.

I aligned with the ajna center in order to access its

solution-creation abilities.

After completing the alignment, I formulated several possible solutions to the problem and implemented what appeared to be the best one (while leaving others open).

The primary focus throughout this outer activity was on performing the inner activity of consciousness in order to help a child. This completely transformed the quality and character of the situation. Billie was frustrated and anxious when I arrived, but calmed immediately when I spoke with him (communicating the quality of the alignment via my words and tone of voice).

The basic procedure is the same in any situation. The organizer begins with an alignment of the consciousness in order. This is how the organizer practices the Law of Relationship.

In chapter 25 we will explore how the business people of the Aquarian age use Divine Order in their practice of the Law of Relationship.

How to Serve Humanity

Chapter 25

Economy and Finance

Part 1

The new type of economist is a practitioner of the creative process who specializes in supplying the flow of mental energy, emotional force, and vital substance.

They supply that flow by performing the creative process. They relate divine purpose to substance, and substance to purpose, much as do the other practitioners of the Law of Relationship. However, their primary focus is on the flow itself—establishing, nurturing, and increasing its quality.

They are concerned with the quality, as quality carries the frequency of consciousness or soul.

They are concerned with right relationship with and within the one life, as misrelationships are seen as the source of blockages to the flow.

They may work in any outer field, but will especially be found in business, finance, and commerce of all kinds.

Wherever found, they may be recognized by their focus on the supply of energy, force, and substance.

Aligning as a Financier

Having aligned with the energy and function of organizers, the next step is to align with the energy and function of economists. In this first section on economy we will take the inner position of the new economist. In the second section on economy we will perform the alignment as an economist:

Sit comfortably, close your eyes, take a deep breath and as you inhale move into your heart.

Perform the usual opening alignment—relaxing your physical body, calming your emotions, focusing your mind, and identifying as the consciousness in the heart.

As the consciousness in the heart, align upward, through the top of the head, with the soul of humanity.

Recognize that you are part of the soul of humanity, and as soul have a relationship with the planetary life.

As the consciousness in the heart, continue the upward alignment, through the soul of humanity, with the abundant supply of the one life.

Aligned with that supply, audibly state the following:

"I stand receptive to the abundant supply of the one life and to its circulation from the overshadowing spiritual soul, into my bodies, and through my bodies to those who stand in need of it within the one life."

(Remain still and undisturbed, for at least 3 minutes,

268

while the supply flows.)

Audibly sound the *"OM"*.

Take a deep breath, and as you release it slowly relax your attention and return to this time and place.

Namaste.

Chapter 25, Part 1

Commentary

The economy of the Aquarian age is absolutely vital to the civilization of that age, and yet many of those who are called on to create that civilization are repelled by the very idea of business, finance, and economy. There are deep reasons for this, and we can only touch on them here.

Generally speaking, in the Piscean age those on the spiritual path had a very deep-rooted, negative attitude toward commerce of all kinds. This negative view ranged from seeing commerce as a distraction to an absolute evil. This view grew out of the emphasis of the age, on aspiring to an abstract (often masculine) ideal. The material world, the things of that world, and the mother aspect or divine substance, were perceived as the opposites of that ideal and thus presumed to be opposed to it.

This was not a fault of the Piscean age or its energies. It was simply a matter of the way humanity responded to those energies because of where we were in our growth and development.

Spiritual seekers commonly responded to the material world by taking vows of poverty, and having as little as possible to do with money. This had two mutually-supporting effects.

It left the fields of commerce open to those who did not have a spiritual focus, and impressed business people with the idea that their work was evil.

It impressed the substance of business and finance, and of the entire economic system, with the idea that it was evil.

Thus impressed, those who worked in the fields of commerce, and the substance with which they worked, accepted the idea that their work was evil and behaved accordingly. The result is a system of commerce in which corporations and individuals behave as though they are separate from the one life, and have no responsibility to that life.

This attitude persists to this day; including among those whose task is to formulate the new economy. It represents a severe misrelationship between humanity and the one life, and must be adjusted, by the practice of the Law of Relationship, before humanity can take its next step. That next step is the development of the new consciousness, in which every human being becomes aware that they are soul. That new consciousness will be developed by the new world civilization, which will be supported by the new economy.

The New Economy

Where the old economy is based on the exchange of physical materials and actions, the new economy is based on the practice of the Law of Relationship. Where the purpose of the old economy is to accumulate goods and services, the purpose of the new economy is to raise the quality of the one life.

The new economy is focused on quality rather than quantity, consciousness rather than form, creative activity rather than accumulation.

The creative activity is of course the conscious practice of the Law. The basic alignment is the same as for all the other new professions. One moves into one's place of focus as soul, aligns upward with the overshadowing purpose, invokes that purpose downward into one's place of focus, projects it outward to the world of appearance, and aligns the world of appearance directly back up with the overshadowing purpose.

The characteristics that distinguish the new business person, financier, or economist include:

The substantial basis of the new economy is the energy, force, and substance of the three lower worlds. The practitioner creates, nurtures, and directs the flow of mental energy, emotional force, and vital substance. They then direct that abundant flow into the physical realm, allowing substance itself to create whatever form best expresses the motivating purpose.

The outer form is created by substance itself, not by the practitioner. The practitioner's primary focus is on the creative activity of consciousness, as that consciousness uses the abundant flow of energy, force, and substance to move purpose downward, outward, and back upward. As a result, relatively little of the practitioner's attention is focused on the resulting physical form or appearance. They are concerned that the form carries the quality of consciousness, and the focus of purpose, but they are not concerned with what the form looks like. Not only do they not envision the form before it appears, but from their perspective it is impossible to do so accurately and any attempt to do so would interfere with the creative process.

One attracts what one needs, rather than accumulating it. When the practitioner perceives an economic need, they immediately begin performing the inner creative process in order to direct a portion of the economy of the one life toward the fulfillment of that need. They use the power of will to motivate and direct that economy, and the magnetic power of love to attract what is needed and to hold all in right relationship.

One's economy is experienced as part of the economy of the one life, rather than apart from it. The practitioner experiences and works within the economy of the one life, appropriating part of its abundant flow and directing it to where it is needed. When blockages to that flow arise, the practitioner looks for their cause in misrelationships between the purpose and the substance of the one life, and works to clear the blockage by adjusting the relationship.

Thus, the essential difference between the old type of business person, economist, or financier is that where the old focused on increasing numbers or accumulating larger amounts, the new focuses on promoting the flow of divine intent into appearance.

During this period of transition from the old to the new

age there is a tendency to assess the flow of energy, force, substance, and appearance in the old numeric terms. An example would include the assessment of a pipeline by the amount of liquid that it can hold at any given moment.

The next step is to realize that the amount that a pipeline can hold at any given moment is less important than the rate of flow—the more rapid the rate of flow, the more material (energy, force, substance, or liquid) flows through the pipeline. This is seen in fiber optic communications. Commonly they upgrade not by adding more cables, but by increasing the rate of flow of data through the existing lines.

In fiber optics, they change to signal lasers that function at a higher frequency. The higher the laser frequency, the shorter the waves of light; the shorter the waves of light, the more data can be included in any particular length of cable at any one moment; in effect, the greater the flow.

The new economist realizes that as they increase the quality of energy, force, and substance, the vibratory rate of that substance increases. More energy, force, and substance can then flow through the channels of the individual, group, and planetary mental, emotional, and vital bodies.

The quality of the mental, emotional, and vital channels also increases, as do the bodies of which they are a part, raising the frequency of the entire instrument.

In this way the new business person, financier, and economist help supply their fellow practitioners, humanity, and the one life, with an economy that transforms the persona, group, and planetary bodies into vehicles of the new consciousness.

This is how the new economist practices the Law of Relationship.

In Part 1 of Chapter 25 we have explored the work and identity of a business person, economist, or financier in the new, Aquarian age. In Part 2 we will explore how to function as an economist in cooperation with all of those with whom one works.

Chapter 25

Economy

Part 2

The new financier uses their alignment to nurture the abundance of the one life. That abundance manifests through the free flow of energy, force, and substance to wherever it is needed. Thus, the new financiers, business people, and economists work to nurture that flow.

The new economists focus the purpose and outline the structure of the flow. The new financiers create abundant sources of energy, force, and substance with which to add to the flow. The new business people create the ordered activities that direct the flow to groups and individuals.

Together, the new economists, financiers, and business people are precipitating the abundance that will support the new world civilization.

Chapter 25

Acting as a Financier or Business Person

Having taken the inner position of an economist, in this second section on economy we will perform the alignment as an economist:

When you recognize a condition of misrelationship within the economy, take a deep breath and as you inhale move into the heart and identify as the consciousness in the heart.

As the consciousness in the heart, recognize that that condition is the outer expression of a mis-relationship with the one life.

Align upward, through the top of the head, to and through the soul of humanity, with that love-wisdom that is divine relationship.

Invoke the consciousness and energy of divine relationship into your heart by silently sounding the *OM*.

As the consciousness in the heart, resonating with right relationship, align upward, through the top of the head, with that divine purpose overshadowing that outer condition.

As the consciousness in the heart, resonating with right relationship and aligned with the overshadowing divine purpose, align outward with that condition of mis-relationship.

Project that overshadowing purpose to that condition by audibly stating the following:

"Standing midway between this condition and its abundant supply, I demand that that supply appear, and with love project it outward to manifest as abundance in the three lower worlds and in the world of affairs." (Remain still and undisturbed, for at least 3 minutes.)

Draw a line of light upward, from the physical brain of the portion of humanity involved, directly to the overshadowing purpose of that condition. (Pause for at least 1 minute.)

Sound the *"OM"* (audibly or silently, depending on the outer situation).

Take a deep breath, and as you release it slowly relax your attention and return to this time and place.

Namaste.

Chapter 25, Part 2

Commentary

In Part 1 we used the terms "economist," "financier," and "business person" almost interchangeably. However, that is as much an overgeneralization in the new age as it was in the old. Each has their particular emphasis within the creative process, and their function within the new economy.

The new economists use the Law to relate with and to bring the overshadowing purpose of the economy into focus, and to relate that purpose with the underlying structure of the economy. They are focused on the underlying structure through which the economy flows.

The new financiers use the Law to draw abundant supplies of energy, force, and substance to wherever it is needed. They are focused on the creative process that drives the flow, and identify with that process rather than with the abundant appearance it creates.

The new business people use the Law to direct the abundant supply into the mental, emotional, and vital activities of the new world civilization. That supply is often contained in a convenient outer form or product. However, the new business people see all physical products as merely convenient containers of the true inner supply. They are focused on the creative process that molds the supply into the thoughts, feelings, and vital energies that will help humanity

How to Serve Humanity

achieve its next step in evolution.

All of these new professions, and their various subsidiary expressions, share a view of the new planetary economy as a flow of mental energy, emotional force, and vital substance.

Building the Structure of the Flow

The new economists do not just observe and evaluate the underlying structure of the economy. While that remains a part of what they do, it is an increasingly smaller part. Like all the new professions their primary focus is moving to performing the Law of Relationship. They are also greatly affected by the transformation of the intellect from a vehicle of sequential organization and number into a vehicle of the new creative process. For the new economists, this means altering not only the focus of their work (from numbers to process) but the method as well.

The new method is, of course, the practice of the conscious creative process. In their case, they formulate the subtle structure (lines or tubes of light) through which the mental energy, emotional force, and vital substance flows. They do this by relating the overshadowing purpose with the embodying condition, and instructing the appropriate substance to build the lines of light connecting the purpose with the need, through which the supply can flow. They do not, however, provide the subtle supply, for that is the task of the new financiers.

Providing the Supply

The new financiers do not just supply financing for

economic ventures. While that remains a part of what they do, the larger part takes place behind the scenes in the subtle realms. The transformation of the creative process, the transformation of civilization and human consciousness, the increasing presence of Aquarian energies, all have affected their profession as much as any other.

In their case, the new financiers use the creative process to magnetically attract, radiate, and direct energy, force, and substance through the subtle structures. They are the ones who set the energies flowing. They use divine will to focus and motivate the economy, divine love to attract and relate it, and divine order to direct it to where it is needed.

When the flow is interrupted due to a misrelationship within the economy, it is the new financiers who step in to clear blockages, adjust the flow, and/or redirect misdirected energies. In fact, a sub-specialty within the new finance will be adjusting economic misrelationships in groups, communities, nations, and the entire planetary life.

Building the Subtle Forms

The new business people do not just supply goods and services. While that remains a part of what they do, most of their work occurs in the subtle realms. The new business people use the creative process to project the new economy into appearance in the three lower worlds (the mental, emotional, and vital realms), and then reflect what is built there into the physical world.

Through business, the new economy will:

Become thought on the mental plane,

Become emotions on the emotional plane,

Become ordered activity on the vital plane, and

Take shape and form in physical matter.

Thus, the new business people are responsible for creating the subtle and physical forms of the new economy. These forms contain the purpose, consciousness, and quality of the new age, and convey that purpose to humanity. And that, in essence, is the purpose of the new world economy.

The new economy provides the energy, force, substance, and forms which all the new professions need in order to perform their functions. It supplies humanity with the energy, force, and substance it needs in order to take the next step in its evolution.

The new economists, financiers, and business people are in turn assisted in and supported by the other new professions, directly and indirectly, as those professions perform their work.

Thus, no matter our profession, all of us have a relationship with the new economy and with the workers in this field. They, like we, are practitioners of the Law of Relationship.

In chapter 26 we will explore how the artists of the Aquarian age use Divine Harmony in their practice of the Law of Relationship.

Chapter 26

Art

Part 1

We are blessed to live at a time of disharmony, when beauty is increasingly rare and treasured; a time when "art" has lost its purpose and is searching for meaning.

Some might say that art has lost its way, and in a sense it has. But this is part of humanity's search for our place in and relationship with the one life. In that quest artists, like all seekers, look both inward and outward.

Having cast off the limitations of the old, Piscean purpose and form, artists can become conscious practitioners of the Law of Relationship—portraying the inner quest, and conveying divine qualities to humanity through thought, feeling, vitality, and form.

Aligning as an Artist

Having aligned with the energy and function of economists, the next step is to align with the energy and function of artists. In this first section on art we will take the inner position of the new artist. In the second section on art we will perform the alignment as an artist:

Sit comfortably, close your eyes, take a deep breath and as you inhale move into your heart.

Perform the usual opening alignment—relaxing your physical body, calming your emotions, focusing your mind, and identifying as the consciousness in the heart.

As the consciousness in the heart, align upward, through the top of the head, with the soul of humanity.

Recognize that you are part of the soul of humanity, and as soul have a relationship with the planetary life.

As the consciousness in the heart, continue the upward alignment, through the soul of humanity, with the harmony of the one life.

Aligned with that supply, audibly state the following:

"I stand receptive to the sound of the one life, aspire to sense the frequency of that silent sound, to understand its meaning, and to then reproduce it harmonically within the three lower worlds, realizing that this harmony is an attribute of the one soul."

(Remain still and undisturbed, for at least 3 minutes,

284

Chapter 26

while the harmony sounds.)

Audibly sound the *"OM"*.

Take a deep breath, and as you release it slowly relax
your attention and return to this time and place.

Namaste.

Chapter 26 Commentary

In the Piscean age, art was a means of illustrating the ideals toward which a group or society aspired. It began with religious art, and then moved to pastoral settings, still life's, and other idealized scenes.

This changed as the incoming Aquarian energies began to be felt. Art grew fractured and abstract as the old idealism broke down and artists turned to illustrating light, motion, and relationships.

This too changed as the Aquarian energies moved toward predominance. The old Piscean purpose and meaning of art disappeared, and it lost all definition. Art increasingly became a means of self exploration and expression—a way of exploring your thoughts, feelings, and identity through creative activity.

Thus, art is becoming a process through which one explores, experiences, and shares the new spiritual path. It is becoming a method of using the Law of Relationship to illustrate the Law of Relationship (among other divine laws, ideas, and energies).

From the perspective of the Aquarian age, art includes anything that conveys a divine quality to humanity—especially the joy, beauty, and harmony of the one life.

An artist is one who adds to that joy, beauty, and harmony, directly or indirectly, by their conscious performance of the Law of Relationship.

Chapter 26

Many artists contribute to harmony indirectly. They illuminate disorder, conflict, or disharmony by creating works that focus and express those conditions. The result may appear ugly, frightening, or repellant, but is a necessary part of the function of art, as it helps us see the disharmony around us. Having experienced and recognized that misrelationship, we can then transform it into harmony and at-one-ment.

Many artists add to the planetary harmony directly. They create works that focus and express right relationship within some portion of the one life. The result is always joyful, beautiful, and harmonious at some level.

Artists create art by practicing the Law of Relationship. They relate the motivating purpose of the planetary life with its mental, emotional, and physical substance. The resulting forms are balanced expressions of will and matter. They exist in harmony with the greater life, and convey something of that harmony to those who experience them.

When an artist practices the Law consciously, performing every stage of the creative process carefully and completely, the resulting work is very powerful. It is very effective at conveying the qualities it embodies to those who experience it.

The new art is effective because it is a living embodiment or expression of a divine quality. It may appear joyful or sad, beautiful or ugly, harmonious or dissonant, but there is a divine quality behind that appearance. The overshadowing divine quality may include:

Divine purpose, power, and will,

How to Serve Humanity

Divine love-wisdom,

Divine intelligence,

Divine harmony,

Divine knowledge,

Divine aspiration, and

Divine order.

While art is most closely associated with harmony, it is not limited to that energy, and may convey any of them. Indeed, an effective piece will include all of the above qualities to some degree, while emphasizing one or two of them.

The artist is able to align with, invoke, and inject these divine qualities into their art because they are in tune with those qualities within their self or soul.

Each of these seven qualities is part of the nature of the self. They are characteristics of the consciousness, and underlying energies of the bodies. That is, the soul *is* divine purpose, power, and will. It expresses that purpose as the "I will to be" of the soul that propels the consciousness into existence.

The soul *is* divine love-wisdom. It expresses that love-wisdom as the "I exist" which is the pure identity of the soul.

The soul *is* divine intelligence. It expresses that intelligence as the "I create" which produces the conscious, creative activity of the self.

288

Chapter 26

The new artist embodies these seven qualities by wielding them in the creative process. They may focus on creating an expression of divine harmony, but will use:

The divine purpose of the one life to motivate their efforts,

Divine love to relate the purpose of their work with those who need it,

Divine wisdom to understand that purpose,

Divine intelligence to develop their creative actions,

Divine harmony to hold all in balance within the one life,

Divine knowledge to attract the information needed to create their work,

Divine aspiration to align their work (both process and product) with the overshadowing divine purpose and plan, and

Divine order to direct the creative process.

In this way, the new artist creates the art that aligns humanity with the one life, and helps raise the entire human kingdom into awareness of itself as soul.

In Part 1 of Chapter 26 we have explored the identity and work of an artist in the new, Aquarian age. In Part 2 we will explore how to function as an artist in cooperation with all of those with whom one works.

How to Serve Humanity

Chapter 26

Art and Culture

Part 2

The new artist uses their alignment to nurture the harmony of the one life. That harmony manifests through the alignment of energy, force, and substance with the planetary purpose. Thus, the new artists work to sound that harmony through and within their every creation.

The new artists bring into focus an overshadowing portion of divine purpose, sound that purpose as a creative word, and impress that silent sound on the thought, feeling, and vital activity of their creation. That creation then becomes a radiant source of that word, sounding it forth to all who experience it, exposing them to the quality, and aligning them with, that portion of divine purpose.

Thus, using the Law of Relationship, the new artists create forms through which anyone may experience some portion of the new path, the new consciousness, and the divine plan of the one life.

Acting as an Artist

Having taken the inner position of an artist, in this second section on art and culture we will perform the alignment as an artist:

When you recognize a condition of misrelationship within the world harmony, take a deep breath and as you inhale move into the heart and identify as the consciousness in the heart.

As the consciousness in the heart, recognize that that condition is the outer expression of disharmony within the one life.

Align upward, through the top of the head, to and through the soul of humanity, with that love-wisdom that is divine relationship.

Invoke the consciousness and energy of divine relationship into your heart by silently sounding the *OM*.

As the consciousness in the heart, resonating with right relationship, align upward, through the top of the head, with that divine purpose overshadowing that outer condition.

As the consciousness in the heart, resonating with right relationship and aligned with the overshadowing divine purpose, align outward with that condition of disharmony.

Project that overshadowing purpose to that condition by audibly stating the following:

Chapter 26

"Standing upon the scales, I sound the word of harmony, and reaching up and out I bring into this relationship that peculiar motion which results in balance".

Draw a line of light upward, from the physical brain of the portion of humanity involved, directly to the overshadowing purpose of that condition. (Pause for at least 1 minute.)

Sound the *"OM"* (audibly or silently, depending on the outer situation).

Take a deep breath, and as you release it slowly relax your attention and return to this time and place.

Namaste.

Chapter 26, Part 2

Commentary

In Part 1 we used the term "artist" to refer to all workers who specialize in using the conscious creative process to nurture planetary harmony. This is an oversimplification.

The new artists may channel joy, beauty, harmony, some other divine characteristic, or even the antithesis or opposite of that characteristic. Their goal is to reveal the divine to those who would not otherwise be able to perceive it. Their method is to create a vehicle that carries and reveals that aspect of the divine. We will discuss that method shortly.

The new art is not limited to what is formally recognized as art, but will be embodied in every aspect of the new culture. The term "culture" has many definitions, but in common usage usually has three meanings:

Excellence in taste: When we say, "They are very cultured." we mean that that individual or group has excellent taste in art, architecture, literature, food, furnishings, etc. This definition focuses primarily on the outer forms of a culture.

The shared attitudes, values, goals, and practices that characterize a group, organization, nation, or people: This focuses on the common emotional feelings of a culture.

Chapter 26

A shared pattern of knowledge, belief, and behavior that grows out of the capacity for symbolic thought and social learning: This includes common customs, beliefs, behaviors, myths, songs, styles, etc. This definition focuses on the common mental thoughts of a culture.[5]

Thus, the term culture has had different meanings depending on whether the focus was on thought, emotion, or physical appearance. Each definition has been just as correct and just as valid, for a culture exists in all three realms. However, these aspects of culture were perceived separately because those who did the perceiving were not integrated. Their minds, emotions, and physical brains functioned separately from each other, with one of them predominant, and the predominant body determined how they saw a culture.

An individual or group dis-integrated in this way is not capable of creating a culture that is aligned and integrated with the one life. Being separated, they can only perceive and create separation. As a result, it is very unwise to teach someone the conscious creative process without first teaching them how to focus as the self or soul in right relationship with the one life. This is a heart center focus, which is followed by the integration of the three aspects of the persona—body, emotions, and mind—in aspiration to the one life.[6]

---

[5] These three definitions of culture are partly based on the "Culture" listing in Wikipedia.

[6] The inner work of *How to Serve Humanity* focuses on developing a heart center alignment. Developing an integrated persona alignment, in aspiration to the one life, is the focus of the upcoming companion course, *How to Save Earth*.

How to Serve Humanity

In the Aquarian age these three aspects of culture will be integrated into one by the conscious performance of the creative process. Artists working in every area of the new world culture will develop integrated mental, emotional, and physical forms that carry and reveal the overshadowing aspect of the divine.

The new artists will work in the areas of:

Divine purpose or leadership,

Divine love-wisdom or healing and education,

Divine intelligence or economy,

Divine harmony or culture,

Divine knowledge or science,

Divine aspiration or religion, and

Divine order or conscious creativity.

Whatever divine characteristic they are working with, or area they are working in, the new Aquarian artists will use the same triangular creative alignment. Recognizing a condition of dis-harmony in the world, they will:

Identify as the consciousness or soul, and move into their point of focus in their instrument.[7]

---

[7] This point of focus may be the heart, brow, or center of the head. We will work with the brow or ajna point in *How to Save Earth*, and with the center of the head or cave center, in *The Nature of The Soul*.

Chapter 26

From the point of focus, align upward, through the top of the head, with the aspect of divinity overshadowing that condition (divine purpose, divine love-wisdom, etc).

Remaining in the point of focus, and maintaining the upward alignment, align outward with the condition:

On the mental plane, aligning the mental energy or thought of that condition back upward directly to the overshadowing aspect of divinity.

On the emotional plane, aligning the force or emotion of that condition back upward directly to the overshadowing aspect of divinity.

On the vital plane, aligning the substance or activity of that condition back upward directly to the overshadowing aspect of divinity.

On the physical plane, aligning the matter or outer form of that condition back upward directly to the overshadowing aspect of divinity.

At each stage, one sounds the creative word of harmony that produces right relationship and balance. One continues to sound that creative word at each level, until the condition moves into harmony on that level, before moving on to the next.

As a result, by the time the artist picks up the tool of their art—brush, chisel, pen, camera, whatever, the inner life of their creation is complete and has merely to be given an outer form or package. Most of humanity may perceive only that outer form, but that form is vital, alive, and effective because of its consciously-created and aligned inner structure.

Working in this way, using the Law of Relationship, the new artists will create art that is far more harmonious and powerful than anything yet seen.

In chapter 27 we will explore how the new media of the Aquarian age will practice the Law of Relationship.

Chapter 27

Science

Part 1

We are blessed to live at a time of revolution, when the old order is being transformed by the magic of the soul.

The consciousness and energies of the Aquarian age are revolutionizing the field of science. The old, isolated, quest for pure knowledge is passing away as scientists begin to discover the one life.

The science of the Aquarian age is based on conscious creativity in cooperation with the planetary life. For the new scientists, knowledge is a tool for understanding and serving the one life, and the quest for knowledge is the quest for better ways to serve.

Aligning as Soul

Our next step is to align with the practice of science. In this first section on science we will take the inner position of the new scientist, or practitioner of divine knowledge. In the second section on science we will perform the creative process as a scientist:

Sit comfortably, close your eyes, take a deep breath and as you inhale move into your heart.

Perform the usual opening alignment—relaxing your physical body, calming your emotions, focusing your mind, and identifying as the consciousness in the heart.

As the consciousness in the heart, align upward, through the top of the head, with the soul of humanity.

Recognize that you are part of the soul of humanity, and as soul have a relationship with the one life.

As the consciousness in the heart, continue the upward alignment, through the soul of humanity, with the one life.

Aligned with the one life, audibly state the following:

"I stand receptive to the divine knowledge of the one life. I am that life."

(Remain still and undisturbed, for at least 3 minutes, while the above sounds.)

Visualize a line of light back up, from the environment, directly to the overshadowing source of purpose in the

300

Chapter 27

one life.

Audibly sound the *"OM"*.

Take a deep breath, and as you release it slowly relax your attention and return to this time and place.

Namaste.

Chapter 27 Commentary

At its heart, science was a method of seeking Truth via knowledge. It began as "Natural Philosophy," and is based on the "Scientific Method." This method has always varied somewhat from one field of investigation to another, has evolved over time, and no two scientists or even experiments by the same scientist will necessarily use exactly the same methods. However, in general, its basic procedures include: observation, hypothesis, testing, theory, and replication. A scientist observes a phenomena, formulates a hypothesis explaining that phenomena, tests that hypothesis, forms a theory explaining the test results, and then publishes the results so that other scientists may replicate the test and prove or disprove the theory.

A fundamental feature of science is its ability to change or self-correct. Most of the theories generally accepted as correct have eventually been proven incorrect and set aside in favor of new theories. Those attached to a fixed ideal of truth see this change as a flaw, while it is actually a feature of any process of transformation.

The consciousness and energies of the Aquarian age are revolutionizing the field of science. The old, isolated, quest for pure knowledge is passing away as scientists begin to discover the one life. Individual researchers have discovered portions of the one life many times, but the field of science was not ready for their discoveries and they were dismissed or discounted. However, in this new age the fact of the larger life is easier to see and accept.

Chapter 27

This dawning awareness of the larger life is opening the door to new scientific observations, hypothesis, experiments, and theories. For instance, science is beginning to recognize that the human energy field is causative to our physical-dense bodies, that the energy field of Earth is causative to our individual energy fields, and that collectively, we in turn are causative to Earth's energy field. We affect Earth and Earth affects us.

This is a few short steps away from recognizing that Gaia really exists.

The science of the Aquarian age is based on conscious creativity in cooperation with the planetary life. The first step in this co-creative process will be the scientific discovery that Earth is a living, sentient, being, "Gaia," and that we (each and all of us) are part of Gaia. This will not come easy.

The revelation of Gaia will be so shocking to the old scientists that many will be unable to accept it. They will resist recognizing Gaia despite any proofs that may be offered. This has happened many times in science, when mounting evidence forces the creation of new theories which, when proven, force change beyond the ability of some scientists to accept.

The new scientists will not only accept Gaia, they will build their work around cooperating with Gaia.

For the new scientists, knowledge is a tool for understanding and serving the one life, and the quest for knowledge is the quest for better ways to serve.

The main difference between the old and the new scientists

will be in their purpose and their relationships.

Their purpose: The goal of science was to know. Obtaining knowledge was its own goal. The purpose of the new science is to reveal Truth via knowledge, and to use that knowledge in service to the one life.

Their relationship: Formerly, "pure" science sought pure knowledge. Attempts to discover knowledge with practical applications were viewed with the same disapproval that fine artists directed toward commercial art. Motivated by the aspiration to serve, the new scientist seeks to discover and apply truth to benefit all.

The new scientist will benefit the one life by practicing the Law of Relationship.

The old Newtonian scientists aspired to be neutral observers. They sought to observe the world without affecting it. In their mechanistic world-view, neutrality was like the neutral gear of a car, disconnected from and unaffected by the world. In human beings this disconnection was not neutrality, but intellectual suppression of their awareness of relationships. That suppression created the appearance of isolation and detachment.

"No man is an island." We live, move, and have our being within the planetary life, whether we are aware of it or not. We may suppress our awareness of that life, but that life and our relationship with it remain.

True neutrality comes not with detachment, but with at-one-ment. Every electrician knows that energetically "neutral" is "ground." Typically, the neutral or ground plug in an electrical socket is attached to a wire that is attached to a metal rod that has been driven into the ground. The ground socket is neutral because it has the same electrical frequency as Earth. Neutral does not mean detached, it means at-one with all.

The intellect or rational mind is very good at perceiving and organizing details, but very poor at seeing relationships. Thus, the more rational science became, the more it focused on isolated specialties, and the more it lost its vision of the whole.

Scientists eventually decided that neutrality was impossible, and (for the type of disconnection they meant) were quite correct. This was proven by a famous set of experiments designed to demonstrate if light was a particle or a wave. One experiment was designed to determine if light was a particle, another to determine if light was a wave. The experiments could not be conducted simultaneously on the same light. Both experiments worked, proving that whether light was a particle or a wave depended on how the observer looked at it.

Thus, simply by the act of observation, the observer changed what was observed. There could be no such thing as a neutral observer who did not affect what they observed. This seemed to be a flaw in the old science, but actually it was the basis for the new science of the Aquarian age.

The new science is based on the fact that the observer changes what they observe. The goal of the new science is to learn how to observe portions of the one life in order to bring about specific changes. The new scientist will:

How to Serve Humanity

Observe a condition within the one life,

Formulate a hypothesis explaining that condition,

Test that hypothesis,

Formulate a theory explaining the test results, and then

Publish the results so that others may replicate the test and use the results to benefit humanity and the one life.

For the new scientist, observation is an act of self awareness and transformation. They are a self-aware fragment of the one life, observing another portion of the same life. They are the one life observing itself. They are a neutral observer because they are identified with the entire life, and their motivating purpose is to serve that life. The alignment the new scientists will use is quite familiar to us. They will:

Observe a condition within the world.

Focus in the heart, and identify with the one life.

Align upward from the heart, with the overshadowing purpose of that condition.

Align outward with that condition.

Align upward, from that condition, directly to its overshadowing purpose.

At-one the condition and its purpose.

306

Chapter 27

Observe until the condition transforms.

This, also, is the practice of the Law.

In Part 1 of Chapter 27 we have explored the work of science in the new, Aquarian age. In Part 2 we will explore how to function as a scientist in cooperation with the one life.

Chapter 27

Science

Part 2

We are blessed to live at a time of disorder, when the old civilization is passing away.

The new scientist stands between the purpose of the one life, and its substance, and formulates their union.

The new scientist is a practitioner of the magic of consciousness who uses the rituals of the scientific method to reveal the secrets and manifest the purpose of the one life.

They use knowledge and ritual to relate that which is with that which could be, and to direct the builders in their work. Having mastered the laws of physical substance, they will move on to reveal those of the vital, emotional, mental, and spiritual realms, and to prove the existence of the Soul and the purpose and function of humanity in the one life. This, also, is the practice of the Law of Relationship.

Chapter 27

Acting as a Scientist

Having taken the inner position of the new scientist, in this second section on the new science we will perform the alignment as a scientist:

When seeking to understand how any thing is related with everything, take a deep breath and as you inhale move into the heart and identify as the consciousness in the heart.

As the consciousness in the heart, aspire to the one life. When that aspiration has reached its height align upward, through the top of the head, to and through the soul of humanity, with the one life.

From the heart, align outward with that thing (condition, situation, person, etc.) that needs adjusting

Focused in the heart, aligned upward with the one life and outward with that thing, invoke that divine love which produces understanding into the heart by audibly sounding the following:

"I invoke divine love into my heart, so that I may understand this condition, and relate it with its purpose, place, and function in the one life."

Audibly sound the *"OM."* (long pause)

Take a deep breath, and as you release it slowly relax your attention and return to this time and place.

How to Serve Humanity

Chapter 27, Part 2

Commentary

The new scientist uses the scientific method to reveal the divine. Rather than focusing on understanding and manipulating matter, they focus on understanding and revealing the one life. Where human beings had been seen as individual physical bodies, mere intelligent animals, they will be revealed as spiritual beings within a great cosmic life.

Many of the existing specialized fields of science will wither as scientists turn from the study of matter to the realization of soul and spirit. In the process, they will create new fields of study and practice, such as the science of right human relations.

This new field of study, like all those that thrive in the Aquarian age, will be a synthesis of three aspects or attributes. Those are:

Studying and focusing divine purpose,

Studying and realizing divine love,

Practicing the magic of consciousness.

In the new science of right human relations, for instance, purpose, love, and magic will be utilized as follows:

Divine Purpose:

How to Serve Humanity

The first step is to assume that whatever one is investigating (in this case, humanity) is a part of and has a purpose within the one life. The old science did not understand this, and as a result missed and misunderstood a great deal. Take, for instance, the vermiform appendix. It was long believed to be an evolutionary remnant with no purpose in modern humanity. However, in recent years it was realized that the appendix is a storehouse of beneficial intestinal bacteria. If illness or poisoning should kill off the beneficial bacteria in the rest of the intestines, the digestive system can be repopulated from the supply in the vermiform appendix. Thus, that organ has a purpose within the larger life of which it is a part.

The new scientist will assume that humanity has a purpose within the planetary life of which we are a part. Not only will their research be based on that foundation, but our purpose will itself be investigated, brought into clear focus, and made known to humanity.

Divine Love:

Another step is to assume that everything, including whatever one is investigating, has a place within the one life. That place is its position in relationship with everything else in the one life.

The ability to perceive how any thing is related with every thing is the result of divine love, for love is the consciousness, energy, and experience of relationship. When we focus in the heart, from the heart with the one life, and invoke divine love into the heart, we gain the ability to know that everything is one thing and that any one thing is part of everything. Thus, the new scientist will cultivate the ability to know love in the heart.

However, the knowing of the heart is universal, but not specific. In order to focus on any one thing, we need to relate with it via the intellect or concrete rational mind. While the intellect is very poor at perceiving relationships, it is very good at examining and organizing individual details. When we focus in the intellect, from the intellect with the one life, and invoke divine love into the intellect, we gain the ability to see how any one thing is related with any other one thing. We see the details, but not the whole. Thus, in addition to the heart alignment, the new scientist will consciously focus in the concrete rational mind.

The heart and the intellect do not understand and tend to conflict with each other. Yet, both are needed if one is to perceive both the whole and the details. Fortunately there is another stage of perception—the observer—that includes and coordinates the heart and the intellect, and the right and the left brains. The observer or "ajna center" is found approximately two inches in front of the forehead, between the brows. The ajna center will be the primary point of focus in the next course in this series, *How to Save Earth*. Because of its integrative function, the new scientist will use the ajna center to both align with the one life, and to regulate the heart and intellect. When they need to understand or relate with something, the new scientist will focus in the ajna, align upward from the ajna with the one life, and outward from the ajna with the intellect and the heart, and invoke that divine love which brings understanding and right relationship.

Thus, the new scientist will invoke divine love in order to understand and to relate with anything and everything.

Magic:

Another step is to assume that by actively relating with anything and everything they can change it—bring the mental, emotional, vital, and physical forms they observe into closer correspondence with the overshadowing divine purpose. Thus, conscious transformation, performing the magic of consciousness, will replace detached observation.

The new scientist not only realizes that everything has a purpose in the one life, and that they can understand the purpose, place, and function of anything, but that if anything is out of its place or not performing its function it can be adjusted so that it moves into its place and takes up its function within the one life.

Adjusting everything that needs it is not the responsibility of the new scientist. Their task is to use the scientific method to identify how to do so. The new scientist will reveal exactly how the creative process works, and how to perform it. However, actually using the creative process to re-create Earth is the collective responsibility of all the new professions.

When applied to the human kingdom, the new science is the science of right human relations. It is the method the new practitioners will use to create peace, to help humanity discover it purpose, move into its place and take up our function in the one life. This, also, is the practice of the Law of Relationship.

In chapter 28 we will explore how the new media of the Aquarian age will practice the Law of Relationship.

How to Serve Humanity

Chapter 28

The New Media

Part 1

We are blessed to live at a time of disunity, when our connections are increasing in number, but growing shallower in depth, when so many voices vie for our attention that they merge into a meaningless white noise.

More and more of that noise is being generated by the new media—social networking, music, video, games, advertising and a growing host of other sites. Most of it consists of individuals and groups sounding off—making their presence, feelings, views, products, and services known to whoever will listen.

Some might say that the new media has fallen far from the first idealistic vision of the net. But if one listens closely, one can find within that noise the still small voice of the awakening soul of humanity.

Having cast off the limitations of the old, Piscean media, the communicators of the Aquarian age can become conscious practitioners of the Law of Relationship—sounding the new word via voice, music, writing, and image.

Aligning as a Communicator

Having aligned with the energy and function of science, the next step is to align with the energy and function of communicators. In this first section on media we will take the inner position of the new communicator. In the second section on media we will perform the alignment as a communicator:

Sit comfortably, close your eyes, take a deep breath and as you inhale move into your heart.

Perform the usual opening alignment—relaxing your physical body, calming your emotions, focusing your mind, and identifying as the consciousness in the heart.

As the consciousness in the heart, align upward, through the top of the head, with the soul of humanity.

Recognize that you are part of the soul of humanity, and as soul have a relationship with the planetary life.

As the consciousness in the heart, continue the upward alignment, through the soul of humanity, with the idea of Truth overshadowing this age..

Aligned with that idea, audibly state the following:

"I stand receptive to the idea of Truth as it is made known to me by the soul. I experience that Truth, understand its meaning, and announce it to humanity."

(Remain still and undisturbed, for at least 3 minutes, while the harmony sounds.)

318

Chapter 28

Audibly sound the "*OM*".

Take a deep breath, and as you release it slowly relax your attention and return to this time and place.

Namaste.

Chapter 28 Commentary

For our purposes, "media" is the means of communicating with the masses. In the Piscean age, the media streams were few, and largely controlled by those with money and power. This was normal and natural, given the types of leadership, organization, and economy of that age. However, media is being transformed as we move into the Aquarian age. The purpose, consciousness, and energies of the age are decentralized and unifying, in sharp contrast to those of the Piscean. In response, new forms of media are constantly appearing, as old forms disappear or adjust in response.

These new forms, often called "new media," are not in themselves what we mean by that term. While appearing in response to the new age, the inner reality of the outer form is not new unless it is an expression of the purpose, consciousness, and energies of the Aquarian age.

We can clarify the distinguishing inner characteristics of the new media by examining its purpose, consciousness, and energies.

Purpose

The purpose of the new media is to communicate the idea, quality, and methods of the new consciousness. Unlike the Piscean age, in which it was often apparently enough to merely describe an ideal, Aquarian media will have to embody the idea, qualities, and methods it seeks to communicate. This is because the goals of the two ages, while complementary (the Piscean is foundational to the Aquarian, and the Aquarian builds on the Piscean) are quite different.

In the Piscean age the ideal was the goal. The media's function was similar to that of John the Baptist. They announced the ideal.

In the Aquarian age the goal is to precipitate divine purpose. The media's function still includes announcing the idea, but now the announcement must itself be an example or embodiment of that idea.

The Piscean ideal was a vision of truth which seekers aspired to know or realize. The Aquarian idea is an archetype of truth which the seeker works to project into the three lower worlds (mental, emotional, and vital), and into the world of affairs. This idea includes:

The new consciousness—the realization, by every member of humanity, that we are soul

The new path of spiritual growth and development

The new world civilization

The new economy

The magic of consciousness—including, of course, the Law of Relationship

The quality includes the state or condition of consciousness itself, and the energies include those of the Aquarian age.

Some of the methods are already listed above. They

include the new: path, civilization, economy, and magic. Their main distinguishing characteristics are: cooperation, synthesis, and magical order.

The work of the new media will be based on the triangular alignment. They will perform that alignment much as do the other new professions. However, their goal will be to relate conditions, in the three lower worlds and the world of affairs, with the overshadowing idea of truth by announcing that relationship. They will announce it.

The main problem the new media is encountering at this point is that it does not know what its purpose is. Without purpose, it lacks direction, and lacking direction falls back on the old persona motivations of physical appetites and emotional desires.

This lack of focused and focusing purpose also leaves the new media vulnerable to the reactionary old forces who would control or restrict it for their own purposes. These attempts to control the new media are hardly surprising, as the old style of leadership sees the new media as a threat to its control. The old style organization sees it as a threat to order, and the old style economy sees it as a threat to its wealth.

Consciousness

Of course, it is the consciousness of the new media that is responsible for wielding the Law of Relationship. As usual, it does so via the conscious performance of the Law using the triangular alignment. In this case (generally speaking), that alignment is:

Chapter 28

From one's point of focus (heart, brow, or center of the head)

Upward to and through the purpose of the new media, to the overshadowing idea of truth

Outward through the specific media, and through that media to the portion of humanity one is serving

Upward from that portion of humanity directly to the overshadowing idea

Of course, this is only a basic outline. The specifics will vary depending on the embodied condition and the overshadowing idea.

The consciousness performing this alignment will increasingly be that of a group. It may be a media group, the media staff of a larger organization, or an individual working on their own in the outer world. But in any case, largely behind the scenes, they will be identified with a group consciousness and performing the inner creative process as that group consciousness.

Energies

The energies on the ascendancy during this Aquarian age are those of conscious creativity and synthesis. The energy of synthesis has the peculiar effect of clarifying polarities before raising them into at-one-ment. Present-day humanity still tends to see polarities as opposing each other—as two political parties opposing each other, two religions opposing each other, two ideals opposing each other, etc. These apparent conflicts disappear as we move our consciousness into a higher state, where poles are seen as dual expressions of one higher reality, and as those outer poles are raised by synthesis into that higher union.

The energy of conscious creativity is the energy used when we perform the creative process. We may use other energies as we perform that process, but the process itself uses the energy of conscious creativity. Also known as the energy of ceremonial magic, and of divine law and order, this energy is itself being uplifted in frequency during this age. As a result, the old, unconscious practice of the Law of Relationship is slowly giving way to the conscious performance of the Law.

The new media will increasingly use these and other energies consciously. Initially much of their work will focus on announcing and unifying the polarities revealed by synthesis. But always, behind the scenes, they will be wielding the Law of Relationship in service to humanity and the one life.

In Part 1 of Chapter 28 we have explored the purpose, identity, and work of a communicator in the new, Aquarian age. In Part 2 we will explore how to function as a communicator in cooperation with all of those with whom one works.

Chapter 28

Media and Communication

Part 2

The new communicator uses their alignment to sound the word of the soul in the three lower worlds and the world of affairs. Their activities may look like those of the old communicators, as the forms of communication will often be much the same. However, the quality and direction of their communication will be quite different.

The quality they sound will be that of the new consciousness of humanity. Thus, anyone seeking that quality will find it in the new media.

The motivation of their communications will be the divine plan of the one life. Thus, anyone seeking direction from a higher source will find it voiced in the new media.

Since the new communicators use the triangular alignment, anyone experiencing spiritual quality or purpose through the new media will be directed upward to the source rather than outward to the communicators. This, also, is the practice of the Law of Relationship.

Acting as a Communicator

Having taken the inner position of a communicator, in this second section on media we will perform the alignment as a communicator:

When you recognize a condition of miscommunication within the world, take a deep breath and as you inhale move into the heart and identify as the consciousness in the heart.

As the consciousness in the heart, recognize that that condition is the outer expression of miscommunication within the one life.

Align upward, through the top of the head, to and through the soul of humanity, with that intelligent activity that is divine communication.

Invoke the consciousness and energy of divine communication into your heart by silently sounding the *OM*.

As the consciousness in the heart, resonating with divine communication, align upward, through the top of the head, with that divine purpose overshadowing that outer condition of miscommunication.

As the consciousness in the heart, resonating with divine communication and aligned with the overshadowing divine purpose, align outward with that condition of miscommunication.

Project that overshadowing purpose to that condition by audibly sounding the following:

326

Chapter 28

"I sound the word of Truth to those who stand receptive to it, and, as they receive it, align them upward with the source of Truth."

Draw a line of light upward, from the physical brain of the portion of humanity involved, directly to the overshadowing purpose of that condition. (Pause for at least 1 minute.)

Sound the *"OM"* (audibly or silently, depending on the outer situation).

Take a deep breath, and as you release it slowly relax your attention and return to this time and place.

Namaste.

Chapter 28, Part 2

Commentary

In Part 1 we indicated that "media" is the means of communicating *with* the masses. This definition is itself rooted in the Piscean age. In the Aquarian age the new media will be the means of communication used *by* the masses. The new consciousness and energies will remove all central controls over media, and transform it into a means whereby anyone may communicate with everyone.

Of course, the Piscean organizations, both private and public, that depend on controlling the media will feel threatened by the apparent loss of control. As a result, they will attempt to exert control over the new media. However, being identified as the form of their organization, they will attempt to exert control over the form and structure of the new media. This will nullify their misdirected and misplaced attempts to exert control.

In order to avoid the attempts to control the new media, the new communicators have merely to maintain their identity as the soul. The soul is completely beyond the control of any external, material agency such as a form-identified organization. Thus, the soul-identified new communicators will always be able to sound the word of the soul to humanity, no matter what may be done to restrict or stop them.

As the Aquarian age progresses, the old ways of working

Chapter 28

will cease to function and Piscean organizations will find themselves experiencing increasing difficulties. Eventually, they will either adapt by moving into the new consciousness and energies, or they will pass away.

All of this may be easier to explain if we use a concrete example.

The New Communicators

Let us imagine a group—not a physical group but a soul group. The members of that soul group share a relationship with a portion of the plan of the one life, and because of that relationship are responsible for manifesting that portion of the plan in the lower worlds.

This is a heavy responsibility. But it is the responsibility of the soul, rather than the persona, and of a group, rather than an individual. Thus, individuals do not become aware of this relationship with the plan until they become aware of their self as the soul. As they become aware as the soul, they become aware that they, as soul, have a purpose and function within the one life—a purpose and function that is shared by a group of souls.

Let us imagine a soul group that is responsible for communicating a portion of the plan to humanity—in this case, a portion related to the new economy. Now, as communicators they are not responsible for formulating the new economy, for teaching humanity how to use it, or for guiding humanity from the old economy into the new. Those are responsibilities of other groups. As communicators they are responsible for communicating the fact of the new economy to humanity.

329

How to Serve Humanity

As a soul group, only a portion of the group will be in physical incarnation at any one time, and most of those in incarnation may never meet. Yet, wherever they are, they will be using the Law of Relationship, via their shared alignment with the plan, to manifest that portion of the plan—in this case, the plan for the new economy.

So, working together as soul, they:

Identify a condition of misrelationship with economy:

This is becoming easier to do as the old economy breaks down and humanity seeks and demands solutions. In this case, let us suppose that one of the misrelationships identified is with money.

The response of the Piscean seeker to money was to renounce it, to simply give it up and have nothing to do with it. This was part of the attempt to drop all attachments to form, and the life of the form, by taking vows of poverty, chastity, and obedience. The goal was to liberate oneself from the material world and ascend into at-one-ment with the one life.

This is a noble ideal, but it left several problems for Aquarian humanity. In the Piscean age, all forms of wealth, including money, were viewed as obstacles to ascension. Because of where humanity was in its growth and development, all obstacles or impediments were seen as bad or evil. Thus, for thousands of years money was seen as a source of evil.

Money, like every other thing, is made of the substance of the one life. The substance of the mental, emotional, and vital planes is divine, and all physical forms are

330

Chapter 28

reflections of that divinity. Thus, the mental energy, emotional force, and vital activity of money is divine. Money is divine substance, given a sacred purpose, in service to humanity.

So long as humanity identifies money as bad, we will be unable to relate with money properly. That misrelationship manifests as:

Accumulating money for selfish purposes, and

Denying ourselves money (consciously or unconsciously) in order to be good.

This polarity often exists in groups and individuals at the same time. It can produce a misrelationship with money so severe that it cripples an individual or group's ability to function economically. This is part of what is happening to humanity now.

From one's point of focus (heart, brow, or center of the head)

Having identified this condition of misrelationship with money, the group of new communicators move into their point of focus, and align upward with the overshadowing idea of Truth. They hold that alignment with the Truth overshadowing that condition until the purpose of that condition clarifies. Then, they slowly move that idea downward, into the mental plane, and radiate that idea outward on the mental plane by silently sounding the OM.

They continue the process of holding the focus and sounding the OM on the mental plane until that idea becomes clear and complete as a thought on that plane.

How to Serve Humanity

Most of the time the communicators are simply trying to see a thought that already exists on the mental plane (having been built by other workers) so they can include that thought in their communications.

When that thought is clear, they move into the emotional plane and sound the Om there, repeating the process and gathering emotional force.

When the emotional force is gathered and ready, they move into the vital plane and sound the Om there, repeating the process and gathering vital substance.

When the vital substance is ready, they move their attention into the physical world of affairs, sound the Om there, and gather the physical forms and activities needed to announce this aspect of Truth to humanity.

Outward through the specific media, and through that media to the portion of humanity one is serving

Having completed the subjective announcement on the mental, emotional, and vital planes, they announce the truth in the physical realm via words, sounds, images, and actions. The words used might include:

"Money is Divine Substance, given shape and form to facilitate the exchange of value."

"Money is Sacred."

Told as part of a campaign to reveal the truth behind the nature and purpose of money, in all its forms.

Upward from that portion of humanity directly to the overshadowing idea

Chapter 28

Thus completing the creative process.

Only in this way can our misrelationship with money be transformed.

Only in this way can the sacred substance of money be redeemed.

Only in this way, by the practice of the Law of Relationship, will the new communicators announce the truth to humanity.

In chapter 29 we will explore how the new world religion will practice the Law of Relationship.

How to Serve Humanity

Chapter 29

The New World Religion

Part 1

We are blessed to live at a time of polarization, when the followers of old religions defend themselves by attacking perceived threats to their beliefs and way of life.

The consciousness and energies of the Aquarian age are transforming religion along with everything else. The old religions of the Piscean age were based on aspiration toward union with the divine. They served their function, to the extent that humanity allowed them to do so, and are now transforming or passing away.

The new world religion of the Aquarian age is based on precipitating the divine into appearance. It begins with union and continues with the practice of the creative process. Thus, the new religion is a method whereby humanity will learn to practice the Law of Relationship in service to the one life.

Aligning as a Cleric

Having aligned with the energy and function of communicators, the next step is to align with the energy and function of the new clerics or religious practitioners. In this first section on religion we will take the inner position of the new religious practitioner. In the second section on religion we will perform the alignment as a religious practitioner:

Sit comfortably, close your eyes, take a deep breath and as you inhale move into your heart.

Perform the usual opening alignment—relaxing your physical body, calming your emotions, focusing your mind, and identifying as the consciousness in the heart.

As the consciousness in the heart, align upward, through the top of the head, with the soul of humanity.

Recognize that you are part of the soul of humanity, and as soul have a relationship with the one life.

As the consciousness in the heart, continue the upward alignment, through the soul of humanity, with the one life.

Aligned with the one life, audibly state the following:

"I, the soul, am part of the one life. I relate with and express that life through every thought, emotion, word, and action."

(Remain still and undisturbed, for at least 3 minutes, while the above sounds.)

336

Chapter 29

Audibly sound the *"OM"*.

Take a deep breath, and as you release it slowly relax your attention and return to this time and place.

Namaste.

Chapter 29 Commentary

For our purposes, "religion" is the means the masses use to align with the divine, externally and internally.

In the Piscean age, the alignment used was the old "L" shaped type.

> The priest, pastor, or other cleric aligned upward to the divine, and outward to their congregation.

> The congregation aligned with the priest, and through the priest with the divine.

Congregations typically needed an intermediary between them and the divine because they were incapable of contacting the divine directly. Those intermediaries included thoughts, beliefs, sacred writings, ritual practices, and clerics. Often, neither the priest nor the congregation knew what they were doing, but depended on theology, faith, writings, and rituals, and considered these sacred (rather than keys or doorways to the divine).

In the Aquarian age, the alignment used is the new triangular type.

> The cleric aligns upward to the divine, outward to their congregation, and upward from the congregation directly to the sacred.

> The congregation aligns directly with the divine, both upward and outward—upward to the overshadowing, unmanifest divinity, and outward to the manifest divinity (in themselves, humanity, and the

rest of the world).

The new congregations may use clerics to coordinate their inner and outer activities, but these clerics will be organizers rather than intermediaries. Those organizers will use the triangular alignment to connect the congregation directly with the divine. The congregation will then align with the divine consciously (both overshadowing and manifest), and call the divine into full appearance. The cleric and congregation will increasingly know exactly what they are doing, and will make conscious use of their minds, emotions, vital bodies, and outer rituals in the creative process.

Rather than being faith-based, the new religion will be based on the practice of the Law of Relationship. Congregations will be taught the basics of the creative process, and how to use the Law as a united group. They will be trained to identify as the soul, contact spiritual energies, and use those energies to invoke divine light, understanding, and purpose.

The beginnings of the new religion may be seen in many congregations today, but they have not yet developed the common motivation, consciousness, and rituals that will unite them in the future.

Motivation

The new religion will be motivated by the purpose and energies of the Aquarian age. As we've discussed, that purpose is to bring humanity to the point where we all realize that we are soul. Soul awareness will become as natural and universal in the human kingdom as individual self awareness is today. The new religion will unite the mass of humanity in invoking our soul into appearance. It will unite us in recognizing the soul in each and all of us.

As noted earlier, the predominating energy of the Aquarian age is the movement of the divine into appearance. Rather than being a motivation, this is the movement itself. The new congregations will be taught to identify as soul, to connect, as soul, with the divine, and to move the divine downward into appearance using the energies of the age.

Consciousness

The new religion will be based on the new consciousness, the increasingly common realization that we are soul. The new congregations will learn to identify as the soul (individually, in small service groups, as congregations, and as humanity). As the soul, they will then perform the magic of consciousness in service to humanity and the one life. This work will unify humanity in consciousness, dissolving the conflicts produced by identification with polarizing forms.

Rituals

The rituals used in the new world religion will be universal in their general outlines. All will be based on the conscious, trained performance of the Law of Relationship.

That conscious, creative process will be performed in a cycle of annual rituals. The most important of these rituals will occur during the twelve Full Moons of each year.

During the first half of the year, these Full Moon

Chapter 29

Rituals will focus on invoking the divine energies.

During the second half of the year, these Full Moon Rituals will focus on manifesting the divine energies.

The most important of these twelve Full Moon Rituals will be:

The Full Moon of Aries (typically in April), in which Divine Love is predominant.

The Full Moon of Taurus (typically in May), in which Divine Purpose is predominant.

The Full Moon of Gemini (typically in June), in which the manifestation of right human relations is predominant.

This cycle of rituals will be cumulative—each cycle will contribute to the intensity and effectiveness of the next. This increasing intensity will:

Raise the awareness, sensitivity, and effectiveness of those involved.

Increase the awareness and sensitivity of all humanity.

Draw more members of humanity to participate in the rituals.

The keynote of all of the Full Moon Rituals is service to humanity and the one life. Their goal, and the goal of the new world religion, is to help humanity take its next step in spiritual growth and development. Its method is to practice that next step in magical rituals based on conscious creativity.

How to Serve Humanity

The practice of these rituals is becoming increasingly common. Eventually they will be found at the core of all religious practice everywhere. This does not mean that all the old religions will disappear, for they will not. But those that continue will adapt to include the new teachings and rituals.

Long before the end of the Aquarian age, the new world religion will be firmly established as the religion of humanity, uniting us in understanding, ritual, and service to the one life.

This, also, is the practice of the Law of Relationship.

In Part 1 of Chapter 29 we have explored the purpose, consciousness, and rituals of the new world religion. In Part 2 we will explore how to function as a cleric or religious practitioner in the new world religion.

Chapter 29

The New World Religion

Part 2

The new religious practitioner uses the Law of Relationship to align their congregation with the divine (both within and outside of their selves).

They begin by helping their congregation realize that they, themselves, are divine—that they are part of the sacred source from which all comes, and that the characteristics of that source are theirs as well. They have but to open to the eternal source within.

This realization of divinity is directed into appearance via coordinated, group rituals, performing the magic of consciousness in ongoing lunar and annual cycles. Via those rituals, the congregations align with the one planetary life, via the divine at the core of their being, then invoke that overshadowing divinity into expression in their lives and in their community, and align their lives with the one life. The congregation then takes that alignment with them as they go about their daily life and affairs. This, also, is the practice of the Law of Relationship.

Acting as a Religious Practitioner

Having taken the inner position of a religions practitioner, in this second section on the new world religion we will perform the alignment as a religious practitioner:

When preparing to facilitate a group alignment with a cycle of service (annual or lunar), take a deep breath and as you inhale move into the heart and identify as the consciousness in the heart.

As the consciousness in the heart, recognize that that cycle is an opportunity for divine purpose to manifest on Earth.

Aspire to the one life, and when that aspiration has reached its height align upward, through the top of the head, to and through the soul of humanity, with the over-shadowing divine energy of the cycle.

Remain still, relaxed, and focused, receptive to the over-shadowing divine energy, for at least three minutes.

Invoke the overshadowing divine energy into your heart by silently sounding the *OM*.

As the consciousness in the heart, resonating with that divine energy, align outward with your service group.

Project that overshadowing divine energy to that service group by formulating it into word-form, and audibly stating it (such as in the following example):

"We invoke Divine Love downward, into our hearts, and through our hearts into the world, uniting all life in Love."

344

Radiate the divine energy outward, through the heart of the group to the local community, and through the local community to the planetary life. (Pause for at least three minutes.)

Draw a line of light upward, from the local community directly to the overshadowing source of divine energy.

Audibly sound the "*OM.*"

Take a deep breath, and as you release it slowly relax your attention and return to this time and place.

Chapter 29, Part 2

Commentary

The new world religion will be, in essence, the method whereby humanity collectively practices the Law of Relationship in their daily life and affairs. We will do this by performing the Law together in repeating annual and lunar cycles.

Annual Cycles

Humanity will perform a complete creative cycle each year, following the solstices and equinoxes. Where we choose to begin the annual cycle is somewhat arbitrary, but here we start with the Winter Solstice.

As we learned in the first section of the course, the creative process has four parts—an ascent, meditation proper, descent, and manifestation. In the new world religion the year will be divided into four parts, in which:

The high or most abstract point occurs at the Winter Solstice (Dec. 21/22).

The descent or precipitation occurs over the six months from the Winter to the Summer Solstices.

The low point or manifestation occurs at the Summer Solstice (June 20/21).

The ascent or aspiration occurs over the six months from the Summer to the Winter Solstices.

Chapter 29

Humanity will repeat this annual cycle each year, gradually raising the quality of its consciousness and the vibratory frequency of its environment.

Lunar Cycles

Within each year, Humanity will also perform a complete creative cycle each lunar month. During this cycle, members of humanity may meet to perform rituals together once each month, once each week, or more often.

Where we indicate that each lunar cycle begins is also somewhat arbitrary, but here we start with the Full Moon. In this case:

The high or most abstract point occurs at each Full Moon.

During the Full Moon period (2-3 days on either side of the exact time), rituals will emphasize focusing the purpose, power, and will of the lunar cycle.

The descent or precipitation occurs over the approximately two weeks from Full Moon to New Moon.

During the two descent weeks, rituals will emphasize precipitating the cycle's purpose into the mental, emotional, and vital planes.

The low point or manifestation occurs at each New Moon.

During the New Moon period (2-3 days on either side of the actual time), rituals will emphasize releasing the mental, emotional, and vital substance to create the outer physical form.

How to Serve Humanity

The ascent or aspiration occurs over the approximately two weeks from New Moon to Full Moon.

During the two ascent weeks, rituals will emphasize aspiring to the overshadowing purpose.

Humanity will repeat this lunar cycle each lunar month, contributing to the gradual increase of the quality of its consciousness and the vibratory frequency of its environment.

Holding the Cycle in Focus

The functions of the new clerics will include:

Holding each cycle in focus.

Aligning each focused cycle with its overshadowing purpose.

Aligning each focused cycle with humanity, and humanity with each cycle.

Facilitating the performance of each cycle, so that:

The cycle remains focused.

The overshadowing purpose and energies of the cycle are invoked by humanity and projected to the planetary life.

In addition to providing training in group performance of the creative process, the main functions of the new clerics will include facilitating the Full Moon and related group service activities.

348

Chapter 29

Services

These group activities will invoke the purpose, consciousness, and energies of the cycles and radiate them to the local community. The purpose of these events is to serve the one life as a group within humanity. Thus, the motivation of the new world religion is to be of service to the one life, and the group events are conscious service activities.

Each service will be a performance of the conscious creative process, using the Law of Relationship, and will therefore be structured as a group performance of that process. The essential elements will include:

Preparing the group instrument: This includes relaxing the physical bodies, calming the emotions, focusing the mind, and integrating the entire persona—all in aspiration to the overshadowing soul of humanity. Depending on the group, this process may include movement, music (listening to or singing), mantra, affirmation, performing an outer ritual (such as lighting candles), oral presentations (such as an inspired sermon), or simply leading the group through the inner process.

Integrating the group consciousness: Once the persona instrument is prepared, the group will identify as humanity performing a service activity for the one life.

Aligning the group with the overshadowing: The integrated group will align upward, through the top of their heads (whether or not that specific language is used is unimportant), with the purpose and energies of that cycle.

349

Aligning the group with the outer world: Maintaining the upward alignment, the integrated group will align outward with the world.

Invoking the overshadowing downward: This will probably be projected as a thought in symbolic word-form, such as: "We invoke the divine love of the one life into humanity, and through humanity radiate that love to all the kingdoms of the planetary life."

Aligning the outer world upward: The integrated group will create an alignment back upward, from the kingdoms of the planetary life directly to the overshadowing source of purpose and energy.

This is a basic outline of a group service of the new world religion. It is at heart a group performance of the creative process. The main functions of the new clerics will include facilitating these services. Of course, this, also, is the practice of the Law of Relationship.

In chapter 30 we will explore how the new magicians will practice the Law of Relationship.

Chapter 30

Spirituality (Synthesis)

Part 1

We are blessed to live at a time of chaos, when the old unconscious creativity is being replaced by the magic of the Soul.

The consciousness and energies of the Aquarian age are transforming the practice of magic. The hidden mysteries of the creative process are being revealed, along with humanity's place and function in the universe.

The new magic of the Aquarian age is based on the creative activity of consciousness, the process by which the Soul brings spirit and substance, divine purpose and divine intelligence, into at-one-ment. This is the purpose and function of humanity in the one life.

Aligning as Soul

Having aligned with the energy and function of the new clerics or religious practitioners, the next step is to align with the practice of magic itself. In this first section on spirituality we will take the inner position of the new magical practitioner. In the second section on spirituality we will perform the creative process as a magician:

Sit comfortably, close your eyes, take a deep breath and as you inhale move into your heart.

Perform the usual opening alignment—relaxing your physical body, calming your emotions, focusing your mind, and identifying as the consciousness in the heart.

As the consciousness in the heart, align upward, through the top of the head, with the soul of humanity.

Recognize that you are part of the soul of humanity, and as soul have a relationship with the one life.

As the consciousness in the heart, continue the upward alignment, through the soul of humanity, with the one life.

Aligned with the one life, audibly state the following:

"I stand receptive to the precipitating purpose of the one life, into my consciousness, through my consciousness into my instrument, and through my instrument into my environment."

(Remain still and undisturbed, for at least 3 minutes, while the above sounds.)

352

Chapter 30

Visualize a line of light back up, from the environment, directly to the overshadowing source of purpose in the one life.

Audibly sound the *"OM"*.

Take a deep breath, and as you release it slowly relax your attention and return to this time and place.

Namaste.

Chapter 30 Commentary

Up to this point we've been discussing the magic of consciousness as a process that will be performed by all the new professions. Each of those new professions—leadership, education, healing, organization, commerce, culture, media, and religion—were distinguished from the old professions by:

Their use of the creative process, in service to humanity, and

A specialized area of service: Leaders provide motivating inspiration, teachers cultivate self awareness, healers promote right relationship, etc.

In each case, the fundamental purpose has been the same—to help humanity take the next step in its growth and development—to become aware that we, each and all of us, are soul. This is true in our final profession as well, but with one small but important difference. There is no specialized area of service, because the magic itself is the service.

Where the other new professions are organizers, communicators, and economists who perform magic, the new magicians specialize in the creative process itself. They are not leaders, clerics, or organizers who practice magic, they are, first and foremost, practitioners of the conscious creative process.

This can be difficult to imagine. Up to now we have considered the new creative process only in the context of

Chapter 30

the other professions. Taking it outside that context leaves us very little to work with. It will perhaps be easier if I give a couple examples, beginning with the recent experience of a Teacher.

The Teacher

Recently a Teacher found that he was going to have to move, and would need a new place to live and work. With no obvious place to go, he aligned with the one life and broadcast into that life his intent to serve humanity as a Teacher wherever he was called to teach. He sounded this call as often as he could for a week, and then (continuing the call) announced the need (for a new place to live and serve) to a small portion of his network. He received three offers, and accepted the one that appeared to be the best fit and greatest opportunity for service.

Arriving in the new location (a midsize community on the edge of a large metropolitan area), he immediately began performing the creative process of building a relationship between the need of that area and his function as a Teacher. With the goal of discovering what quality and character of teachings were needed, he began visiting a wide variety of local groups and meetings—spiritual business meetings, new-thought churches, meditation classes, writer's groups, etc. Holding the intent to be of service, he went for long walks around the local communities, acclimating to the local energies, exploring local shops, parks, libraries, etc. Often opportunities arose to talk with people, and he introduced himself as new to the area, asked questions anyone would ask in that situation, and traded business cards when appropriate.

How to Serve Humanity

After a month, word began to get around that an experienced "meditation teacher" was in town. He began to meet people who had already heard of him, and to bump into people around town that he had already seen or met. He was becoming known and recognized as a Teacher, while building demand for his service. He would soon be ready to begin holding introductory classes.

This is an example of how the new type of Teacher goes to a new area and takes up his work. Now, let's look at a similar example of a magician.

The Magician

Imagine a magician in the same position as the Teacher. Upon realizing that she will soon need a new place to live and work, and with no apparent place to go, she performs the inner creative process to announce her availability within and to attract her next step in service to the one life. As opportunities appear she continues to perform the inner work, making no decision until she has completed a full creative cycle. When the cycle is complete, she identifies as the soul, aligns upward with her purpose within the one life, outward with the opportunities, and aligns those opportunities upward with the divine plan. Whatever opportunity she resonates with the most while holding that alignment, she accepts.

Arriving in the new location, she immediately begins performing the creative process of building a relationship between the need of the area and her function as a magician. With the goal of discovering what quality and character of magic is needed, she:

Chapter 30

Aligns with and invokes the overshadowing purpose of the area.

Aligns with the embodied condition of the area in the mental, emotional, and vital realms.

Aligns with the consciousness of the area, and contemplates the character and quality of its relationship with the overshadowing purpose and embodied condition.

She performs a complete creative cycle for each of these, and explores the community while doing so.

She pays particular attention to the motivations of the people while aligning with and invoking the purpose.

She pays particular attention to the activities of the people while aligning with the embodied condition.

She pays particular attention to the quality of brain awareness of the people while aligning with the consciousness.

She will walk around the area, explore local shops, parks, libraries, city centers, civic meetings, etc., much as the teacher did, but with a vital difference. Her point of identity is as a magician, not as a Teacher who is practicing magic. Where the teacher looked for what needed to be taught, the magician looks for what magic needs to be performed.

In all the other new professions, the conscious creative process is the central tool used in the practice of that profession. However, for the new magician performing the magic of consciousness *is* their profession.

How to Serve Humanity

In the situation described in these stories:

The new Leader looks for the type of inspiration that is needed.

The new Teacher looks for the type of awareness that is needed.

The new Healer looks for the type of right relationship that is needed.

The new Organizer looks for the type of order that is needed.

The new Economist looks for the type of economy that is needed.

The new Artist looks for the type of insight that is needed.

The new Communicator looks for the type of understanding that is needed.

The new Magician looks for the type of creativity that is needed.

The specialized area of service of the magicians is the magical process. Like the others they perform that process in service to the one life. Unlike the others, their profession is not yet established in the world civilization. This will come as the new practitioners create the new civilization.

In Part 1 of Chapter 30 we have outlined the identity of the new magician. In Part 2 we will explore how to function

Chapter 30

as a magician, and help the other new professionals create the new world civilization.

How to Serve Humanity

Chapter 30

Spirituality / Synthesis / Magic

Part 2

We are blessed to live at a time of disorder, when the old civilization is passing away.

The new magical practitioner stands between the old and the new, and uses the Law of Relationship to unite that which is with that which could be.

The new magical practitioner stands as the consciousness or soul—aligned upward with the divine plan, outward with the world, and upward from the world to the plan.

They hold that alignment while moving within the world, relating all they encounter with its purpose, place, and function in the one life. Everything they encounter is changed. Consciousness or form, individual or group, all is transformed through alignment with the motivating purpose of the one life. This, also, is the practice of the Law of Relationship.

Acting as a Magical Practitioner

Having taken the inner position of a new magical practitioner, in this second section on the new magic we will perform the alignment as a magician:

When preparing to act within the world, take a deep breath and as you inhale move into the heart and identify as the consciousness in the heart.

As the consciousness in the heart, recognize that that action is an opportunity for divine purpose to manifest on Earth.

Aspire to the one life, and when that aspiration has reached its height align upward, through the top of the head, to and through the soul of humanity, with the overshadowing divine purpose.

Remain relaxed, and focused, receptive to the overshadowing divine purpose.

Invoke the overshadowing divine purpose into your heart by sounding the *OM*.

As the consciousness in the heart, resonating with that divine purpose, align outward with the condition or conditions around you.

Imagine that divine purpose radiating downward into and outward from your heart, to that condition.

Draw a line of light upward, from that condition directly to the overshadowing source of divine purpose.

362

Chapter 30

Holding that triangular alignment, from the overshadowing divine purpose, to your heart, out to that condition, and back up to the overshadowing purpose, sound the *"OM."*

Take a deep breath, and as you release it slowly relax your attention and return to this time and place.

This technique may be performed while participating in, observing, or contemplating an activity or condition, or while simply walking around and radiating into the environment. The OMs may be silent or audible, depending on the circumstances. When using this or any other technique involving people, radiate only into their aura, where the energy is available to them if they accept it, and will enter their center system at their proper time, center, and rate. Never impress an energy on someone without their permission. Simply make it available to them.

Chapter 30, Part 2

Commentary

The new magic will, in essence, be the method whereby humanity creates the new world civilization. That civilization will be based on the conscious practice of the creative process, by all of the new professions discussed thus far, and by those professionals whose specialty is the practice of that magic.

For the specialists in magic, the creative process is what they do, as well has how they do it. Where a leader will *lead* by performing the magic of consciousness, a magician will *align* by performing the magic of consciousness. Their goal is not to lead, teach, or heal, but to establish a persistent alignment.

They hold that alignment while moving within the world, relating all they encounter with its purpose, place, and function in the one life. Everything they encounter is changed. Consciousness or form, individual or group, all is transformed through alignment with the motivating purpose of the one life.

All the new practitioners hold an alignment as constantly as they can. This broadcasts the energies of their profession into their environment, and attracts opportunities to practice the Law as that profession. A leader will attract opportunities to lead, a teacher to teach, a healer to heal, etc.

Chapter 30

A magician, however, is in a somewhat different position. Almost every situation they encounter is in some way an expression of a misrelationship with divine purpose, expressing that purpose more or less incompletely or inaccurately. Sometimes a form may have been a fairly accurate expression of divine intent when that form was created, but the one life has moved on and the form has not, leaving it out of step with the current intent. The more inflexible a form is, the less amenable to change, the more it will grow out of alignment with divine intent as time passes.

This is where the new magician applies their function. Whenever consciousness has become attached to a form, the creative abilities of that consciousness work to maintain that form as it is. The magician uses the Law of Relationship to free the consciousness from that form. They free the consciousness by:

Relating divine purpose to that form: Impressed with a new motivating purpose, the form responds by changing its pattern of activity to match the new or renewed purpose. This includes the mental, emotional, and vital patterns, as well as the outer form or appearance. If the patterns or form are flexible enough, they adapt to the new impression. If they are unable to adapt, they shatter and new patterns and forms are created to replace the old. If the alignment is dropped and the creative process ends at this point, then the new patterns and forms will stop changing, become old and inflexible in turn, and eventually be changed or replaced. However, the new practitioner, particularly the new magician, does not stop there.

Relating the form to divine purpose: The first step created an alignment from the divine purpose and plan to the magician, and through the magician to the pattern. This is a temporary alignment, created and held by the practitioner. The next step creates an alignment from the pattern directly to the divine purpose and plan. When inscribed clearly, strongly, and persistently enough, this alignment becomes permanent, and remains as long as the pattern's divine purpose remains incomplete or unfulfilled.

When a pattern of activity (and through that pattern its outer form) has a persistent alignment with the divine plan, then that pattern does not crystallize. It remains fluid and flexible, continuously relating the need or embodied condition with the overshadowing purpose or potential. As a result, instead of crystallizing, the outer form remains relatively fluid as well, changing its appearance as needed. Of course, this does not mean that a physical form will suddenly transform itself into something else entirely. It simply means that physical forms will be built with change in mind, rather than the polarity of permanence and obsolescence.

In order for the patterns and forms to remain fluid, the consciousness using them needs to remain identified with and as the consciousness performing the creative process.

When the consciousness identifies *with* its creation, the creative process stops. This occurs when the soul becomes attached to a possession, as in "this is my car," "this is my favorite shirt," or "this is what I think."

When the consciousness identifies *as* its creation,

the creative process stops. This occurs when the soul moves into a form, loses its self awareness, and takes on the form as its identity. The most common example is the experience of the persona instrument as who and what we are.

In either case, when the consciousness identifies with or as its creation, the conscious creative process stops and the form crystallizes. The more rigidly identified the consciousness is, the more inflexible the form.

The new magician changes this by realigning the trapped consciousness and crystallized substance with their purpose, place, and function in the one life.

The consciousness is gradually released from the crystallized form.

The form is gradually released from the mis-identified consciousness.

This is the work of the new magician—to liberate both form and consciousness by aligning them with the divine purpose and plan. This also is the practice of the Law of Relationship.

This completes the chapters of *How to Serve Humanity*. All that remains is the Afterword, in which we will outline everything we have covered in *How to Serve Humanity*, and prepare for the next course in this series, *How to Save Earth*.

How to Serve Humanity

Afterword

We are blessed to live at a time when humanity has created a host of world crises that can only be solved via the Law of Relationship.

This has been the fundamental theme of this course, and is the response to the question of its title: How to Serve Humanity?

By practicing the Law of Relationship.

We began our quest for this answer in Part 1 with an exploration of The Crisis of Awakening. In this section we explored:

Awakening Your Purpose

Awakening Your Awareness

Awakening Your Personality

Awakening Humanity

Leaping Into At-one-ment

The Illusion of Isolation

Unlocking Your Creative Potential

In the process, we learned to focus in the heart, and dedicate our body, emotions, and mind to the one life. Thus prepared, we began our practice of the Law of Relationship.

We continued our quest, in Part 2, with an exploration of The Law of Relationship. In this section we explored:

How to Serve Humanity

Releasing Your Power

The Power to Create

Creative Activity

The Soul of Creativity

Serving the Planetary Life

Awakening to the Planetary Life

Awakening One's Place and Function Within the Planetary Life

Aligning the Planetary Purpose

Aligning Planetary Spirit and Matter

Aligning the Personality

Aligning Planetary Matter and Spirit

Performing the Creative Process

Taking up Your Place and Function in The Planetary Life

In the process, we learned to perform the Law of Relationship, took responsibility for the capacity of our heart-focused alignment, and aligned with the various methods of using that capacity in service to the one life. Thus prepared, we began our exploration of the various fields of service.

Our quest continued in Part 3, with an exploration of how to serve the one life by Performing the Creative Process in various professions. In this section we explored:

Leadership

Afterword

Education

Healing

Organization

Commerce

Art

Media

Science

Religion

Spirituality, Synthesis, or Magic

Our quest pauses here, with the heart alignment ready to perform the work, major fields of service identified and described, and all of humanity ready and waiting. You may end your studies here, having learned a great deal, or you may continue the quest, taking up the opportunity offered by doing whatever you feel called to do in service to humanity. If you leave the decision to your heart, you will find that it knows what to do next.

While this course is done, our quest continues. While we have here explored our individual purpose, identity, and functions as souls in the one life, we have not yet explored the purpose and functions of humanity as a whole. The kingdom of humanity has a definite and essential role within the planetary life, and that function depends and is based on the practice of the Law of Relationship.

However, before humanity can recognize its purpose and take up its function, it must take its next step in the evolution of its consciousness. We must, each and all of us, realize that we are a soul within the one life.

How to Serve Humanity

The method of soul realization will be a new civilization, built by the conscious creative process, using the Law of Relationship. All the new professions described above are part of this new civilization, and will both come into appearance with and help create it.

As should be obvious to anyone who is paying attention, the old Piscean civilization is passing away. Humanity is caught up in both attempting to preserve its forms, and in creating something new—little understanding what is happening or why. In *How to Serve Humanity* we explored the nature and methods of the new practitioners who will help form that new civilization. In the next course in this series we will explore how to build the new civilization. That course will be called: *How to Save Earth*.

In the meantime, we close this course with another technique based on practicing the Law, in this case it is designed to help you invoke your new profession, the one to which you have felt the most attracted, into appearance.

Creating Your Function
Within the One Life

The next step is to invoke our function into appearance:

Sit comfortably, close your eyes, take a deep breath and as you inhale move into your heart.

Relax your physical body.

Calm your emotions.

Focus your mind.

Identify as the consciousness in the heart.

As the consciousness in the heart, recognize that you are particularly attracted to one of the new professions:

Leadership, or

Education, or

Healing, or

Organization, or

Commerce, or

Art, or

Media, or

Science, or

Religion, or

Magic

How to Serve Humanity

From the focus in the heart, audibly state the following:

"I invoke this new profession into appearance in my life and affairs, in service to the one life."

Audibly sound the *'OM'* radiating that joy, beauty, and harmony into your environment.

Take a deep breath, and as you release it slowly return to this time and place.

Continue aligning with your new profession, and radiating joy, beauty and harmony into your environment, as you go about your life and affairs.

Further information on *How to Serve Humanity, How to Save Earth, The Nature of The Soul,* and related books and classes are available at:

Blog (information on classes and events): http://howtoservehumanity.com/

Publisher's site (information on related books): http://preparationpress.com/

Author's site (additional information on the Law of Relationship): http://www.gknape.com/